Desert Experimental Range:
Annotated Bibliography

E. Durant McArthur
Stanley G. Kitchen

 United States Department of Agriculture / Forest Service
Rocky Mountain Research Station
General Technical Report RMRS-GTR-312WWW

October 2013

McArthur, E. Durant; Kitchen , Stanley G. 2013. **Desert Experimental Range: Annotated bibliography**. Gen. Tech. Rep. RMRS-GTR-312WWW. Fort Collins, CO: U.S. Department of Agriculture, Forest Service, Rocky Mountain Research Station. 52 p.

Abstract

Entries qualify for inclusion if they were conducted in whole or part at the Desert Experimental Range (DER, also known as the Desert Range Experiment Station) or were based on DER research in whole or part. They do not qualify merely by the author having worked at the DER when the research was performed or prepared. Entries were drawn from the original abstracts or summaries when those were included in the original document. The conclusions are those of the original authors. Likewise, (1) taxonomic treatments are those of the original authors with our occasional annotations for clarification and (2) tense is that of the original. However if the original was presented in first person point of view it was modified to third person point of view to provide internal homogeneity in the document.

Keywords: Desert Experimental Range, Desert Range Experiment Station, salt desert ecosystem, Great Basin desert, North American cold desert, desert ecology, rangeland management, disturbance ecology, invasive species

Authors

E. Durant McArthur, Emeritus Scientist, U.S. Department of Agriculture, Forest Service, Shrub Sciences Laboratory, Rocky Mountain Research Station, Provo, Utah.

Stanley G. Kitchen, Research Botanist, U.S. Department of Agriculture, Forest Service, Shrub Sciences Laboratory, Rocky Mountain Research Station, Provo, Utah; Scientist-In-Charge, Desert Experimental Range.

Desert Experimental Range: Annotated Bibliography

E. Durant McArthur and Stanley G. Kitchen

Introductory Note: Entries qualify for inclusion if they were conducted in whole or part at the Desert Experimental Range (DER, also known as the Desert Range Experiment Station) or were based on DER research in whole or part. They do not qualify merely by the author having worked at the DER when the research was performed or prepared. Entries were drawn from the original abstracts or summaries when those were included in the original document. The conclusions are those of the original authors. Likewise, (1) taxonomic treatments are those of the original authors with our occasional annotations for clarification and (2) tense is that of the original. However if the original was presented in first person point of view it was modified to third person point of view to provide internal homogeneity in the document.

Acknowledgments: The authors are grateful for reviews of earlier versions of this manuscript by David Anderson, National Security Technologies; James Bowns, Emeritus Professor, Utah State University and Southern Utah University; Warren Clary, formerly Scientist-in-charge, Desert Experimental Range; and Barbara Wachocki, Weber State University. Each reviewer has insight from research experience at the DER. The authors are also grateful to science librarians Mike Goates of Brigham Young University, Laura Bojanowski of the USDA Forest Service Rocky Mountain Research Station, and Laura Hutchinson of the USDA Forest Service Northern Research Station who were helpful in obtaining many of the documents included in this work.

The Desert Experimental Range (DER) was established in 1933 when President Herbert Hoover withdrew 225 square km (87 square miles) from the public domain "as an agricultural range experiment station." The DER is located primarily in Pine Valley, Millard County, Utah (USA); one of the many dry basins characteristic of the Great Basin Ecoregion of western North America. About 75 percent of the DER is occupied by coalescing alluvial fans and the flat valley bottom distinguished by the mostly bare remnant of a small Pleistocene lake. The balance of the area is covered with rocky hills where extensive Paleozoic limestone, dolomite, and quartzite and to a lesser extent Cenozoic igneous extrusions are exposed. Elevations range from 1547 m (5074 ft.) at the valley floor to 2565 m (8413 ft.) at the top of Tunnel Spring Mountain.

Climate at the DER is that of a temperate desert with cold winters and warm summers. Mean January and July temperatures are –3.5 °C (26 °F) and 23.3 °C (74 °F), respectively with a mean daily range in temperature of 18 °C (32 °F), though daily summer swings of 28 °C (50 °F) are common. Mean annual precipitation at lower elevations is 157 mm (6.2 in.), about half of which falls during the primary growing season of May through September. Precipitation at upper elevations can be as much as 50 percent higher than valley locations.

The predominant vegetation is the salt-desert shrubland type. Dominant species are short-statured shrubs or subshrubs from the Chenopodiaceae and Asteraceae families and both cool season (C_3) and warm season (C_4) perennial grasses. Numerous forbs, grasses, shrubs and succulents (cacti) including 10 local endemics and representing 40 plant families complement and enrich the dominant native flora. Variations in community composition reflect the influence of local soil characteristics. Taller shrubs and drought-tolerant conifers (juniper and piñon pine) become important at higher elevations. A small number of introduced, invasive annuals impact stability through their effects on ecosystem composition and processes.

Research foci have evolved since establishment reflecting changing scientific and societal interests. One can quickly assess the range of publication outlets and breadth of studies completed by examining the indices included in this compilation. Long-term meteorological and vegetative data sets are maintained by the Rocky Mountain Research Station. The intent of this work is to bring together synopses of the 99 publications to date referable to the DER. It is hoped that this work will facilitate efforts to uncover and apply past contributions while stimulating interest in future opportunities for knowledge discovery and application.

01. Adams, Mary Beth; Loughry, Linda; Plaugher, Linda. 2004. Experimental forests and ranges of the USDA Forest Service. Gen. Tech. Rep. NE-321. Newton Square, PA: Northeastern Research Station. 178 p.

The Desert Experimental Range is among the inventory listed in this report. The USDA Forest Service has an outstanding scientific resource in the 77 experimental forests and ranges that exist across the United States and its territories. These valuable scientific resources incorporate a broad range of climates, forest types, research emphases, and history. This publication describes each of the research sites within the experimental forest and range network, providing information about history, climate, vegetation, soils, long-term data bases, research history and research products, as well as identifying collaborative opportunities, and providing contact information.

02. Alados, C. L; Emlen, J. M, Wachocki, B.; Freeman, D. C. 1998. Instability of development and fractal architecture in dryland plants as an index of grazing pressure. Journal of Arid Environments 38: 63-76.

Developmental instability has been used to monitor the well-being of natural populations exposed to physical, chemical and biological stressors. In this report developmental instability is used to assess the impact of grazing on *Chrysothamnus greenii* and *Seriphidium novum* (= *Artemisia nova*) shrubs, and *Oryzopsis hymenoides* grass, common in the arid Intermountain West of the U.S.A. Statistical noise in allometric relations was used as an indicator of developmental instability arising from grazing-induced stress. Unpalatable species that are not grazed (*C. greenii*) and species that are dormant during the winter-spring grazing period (*O. hymenoides*) show lower allometric variability under high grazing pressure. Palatable species (*S. novum*) exhibit high developmental instability under low and high grazing pressure.

03. Alzérreca-Angelo, Humberto. 1996. Spatial and temporal dynamics of plant populations in salt-desert shrub vegetation grazed by sheep. Logan, UT: Utah State University. 292 p. Dissertation.

The effects of moderate sheep grazing on a shadscale plant community at the Desert Experimental Range, southwestern Utah, U.S.A. was examined using a 59-year data set with two grazing treatments (yes vs. no), two season (spring vs. winter), and two soil types (loamy-skeletal vs. coarse-loamy). Precipitation, total species cover, annuals, shrub survival, seedling recruitment, plant succession, and plant spatial relationships were considered. Precipitation showed high variability (CV = 31%) masking short-term cycles, resulting in study intervals with average (1935-1958), dry (1958-1969), driest (1969-1975), and wet (1980-1994) regimes. Total cover in both grazed and ungrazed pastures increased between 1935 and 1975 before decreasing to 1994. Treatments diverged with time, however, so cover was higher in ungrazed pastures in 1975 and 1994. Individually, *Atriplex confertifolia* decreased from 1958-1994 and *Ceratoides lanata* from 1975-1994. *Artemisia spinescens* increased in ungrazed pastures from 1935-1994, while remaining very low in grazed pastures. Grasses increased from 1935-1994 with little grazing effects. Annuals increased from absence in 1935 to 63% frequency in 1994; precipitation may be related to this increase. Grazing and soil type had few long-term or short-term effects on shrub survival. Similarly, only *C. lanata* showed a microhabitat effect, with greater seedling survival in vegetated than open patches. Seedling recruitment was positively correlated with precipitation. Only *A. confertifolia* recruitment responded to grazing; it was higher in grazed pastures. A fuzzy graph analysis showed a moderate grazing effect on succession. Clumped distributions were common and were unaffected by grazing but increased in wet years. Plant establishment occurred disproportionally in sites occupied or formerly occupied by plants, suggesting facilitation. Negative interference, however, was suggested by new recruitment occurring further from larger existing individuals. Moderate grazing had little effect on spatial relationships. The multivariate approach yielded broader conclusions than any individual factors. Although some factors showed more grazing effects than others, grazing could not completely explain observed changes; climate and inherent plant attributes must also be considered. Management at moderate grazing levels may only play a limited role in shadscale communities.

04. Alzérreca-Angelo, Humberto; Schupp, Eugene W.; Kitchen, Stanley G. 1998. Sheep grazing and plant cover dynamics of a shadscale community. Journal of Range Management 51(2): 214-222.

Despite extensive coverage and long-term use, the extent to which shadscale [*Atriplex confertifolia* (Torr. & Frem.) Wats] community dynamics are driven by grazing rather than by climate and inherent plant characteristics is unresolved. An analysis of a 59-year data set from then Desert Experimental Range, southwestern Utah, with the objective of discriminating between grazing and non-grazing effects on cover dynamics was undertaken. Canopy cover of 9.3 m^2 (5 x 20 ft) plots were estimated in 1935, 1958, 1969, 1975, and 1994. Treatments were time (five dates), grazing, (ungrazed versus grazed), and season (spring versus winter). Time was significant; total cover initially increased following release from uncontrolled grazing and improvement of climate (1935-58, P < 0.001), remained unchanged over the following dry interval (1958-69 < P = 1.000), increased over a drier interval (1969-75, P , 0.001), and then decreased dramatically over the final wet period (1975-1994, P < 0.001). Grazing was also significant (P < 0.001), but cover of ungrazed plots exceeded that of grazed plots only in 1975 and 1994 (P ≤ 0.033). The 6 dominant species showed varying responses to grazing and time, with some responding primarily to grazing (e.g., budsage, (*Artemisia spinescens* D.C. Eaton in Wats.) and others responding primarily to time (climate, longevity, etc., e.g., Indian ricegrass, *Oryzopsis hymenoides R. & S).* Similarly, seasonal effects were not universal. Shrub cover initially increased and then declined dramatically while grass cover monotonically increased. Results suggest that release from uncontrolled grazing coupled with improving climatic conditions were responsible for initial recovery of the community, but that over time, climate and inherent plant traits (e.g., longevity, establishment ecology, etc.) became relatively more important. For total cover and for many individual species, continued grazing affected the rate more than the direction of vegetation change.

05. Anderson, David C. 1978. Cryptogamic soil crusts: factors influencing their development in Utah deserts and their recovery from grazing on Utah winter ranges. Provo, UT: Brigham Young University. 80 p. Dissertation.

The relation of some soil characteristics to cryptogamic crust development, the effects of grazing on cryptogams and time of recovery from damage by grazing were examined at several sites in arid regions of Utah, including the Desert Experimental Range. Electrical conductivity, soil texture and soil phosphorus were found to be correlated with well-developed cryptogamic crusts. Total cryptogamic cover and the number of cryptogamic species were significantly reduced by domestic grazers. When grazing is removed, cryptogamic crusts reestablished within 14-18 years. The incorporation of soil stabilizing, cryptogamic soil crusts into range and management considerations would strengthen the science of range management on arid ranges.

06. Anderson, David C.; Harper, Kimball T.; Holmgren, Ralph C. 1982. Factors influencing development of cryptogamic soil crusts in Utah deserts. Journal of Range Management 35(2): 180-185.

The relation of some physical and chemical soil characteristics to cryptogamic crust development was determined from sites in semi-desert regions of southern Utah, including the Desert Experimental Range. The effects of grazing on cryptogamic crust development were also examined. Electrical conductivity, percentage silt, and soil phosphorus were found to be correlated with well-developed cryptogamic crusts. Both total cryptogamic cover and the number of cryptogamic species decreased under grazing pressure. The management of rangelands, especially in arid regions, would be strengthened by understanding the role of cryptogamic crusts and considering them in range management decisions.

07. Anderson, David C.; Harper, K. T.; Rushforth, S. R. 1982. Recovery of cryptogamic soil crusts from grazing on Utah winter ranges. Journal of Range Management 35(3): 355-359.

Range exclosures located throughout Utah in cool desert shrub communities, including the Desert Experimental Range, were analyzed to determine, (1) the response of cryptogamic crusts to grazing, (2) soil variables that influence the development of cryptogamic crusts and (3) the time needed for reestablishment of cryptogamic communities after disturbance. The amount of lichen, moss and algal cover was found to be considerably reduced by domestic grazing. Sites with moderate to high as opposed to light cryptogamic cover were characterized by significantly heavier textured soils and greater salinity. Cryptogamic cover increased from 4% to 15% during the first 14-18 years of exclusion from grazing, but increased only 1% during the next 20 years. Reestablishment of a cryptogamic crust occurs in at least 14-18 years and possibly sooner.

08. Anderson, David C.; Rushforth, Samuel R. 1976. The cryptogamic flora of desert soil crusts in southern Utah, U.S.A. Nova Hedwigia 28: 691-729.

A total of 81 cryptogams were identified from 34 crust samples from southern Utah deserts, including the Desert Experimental Range. Fifty-eight of these were algae, 11 blue-green algae, 1 green alga, 1 euglenophyte, and 45 diatoms. Six species of mosses (all from the family Pottiaceae) and 17 lichens (12 terricolous and 5 saxicolous) were identified.

09. Anderson, R. Ernest. 1980. Notes on the Cenozoic structural history of the Tunnel Spring Mountains area, Western Millard County, Utah. GPO 855-175. Washington, DC: U.S. Department of the Interior, Geological Survey, Government Printing Office. 24 p.

The construction of cross-strike structure sections combined with stratigraphic studies of exposed Cenozoic rocks and clastic deposits on the flanks of the Tunnel Spring Mountains of the Desert Experimental Range and adjacent areas shows that the region was the loci of several episodes of deformation since early Oligocene time. Whatever deformation occurred in the Tunnel Spring Mountains prior to that time left no record either of strong topographic or structural relief of significant stratal rotation. Three main episodes of deformation are recognized. These are: (1) accumulation of coarse clastic strata together with volcanic strata of Tunnel Spring Tuff during the early Oligocene; (2) deformation that probably involved strong vertical displacement on faults, produced highlands that shed coarse clastic debris and landslide sheets during the middle to late Miocene; (3) possibly beginning in Miocene but extending into Pleistocene the Tunnel Springs Mountains area was involved in two or more phases of normal faulting that produced displacements and stratal rotations of all strata.

USDA Forest Service Gen. Tech. Rep. RMRS-GTR-312WWW. 2013

6

10. Baugh, Tom. 1981. Research on the desert. Ogden, UT: Forestry Research West. U.S. Department of Agriculture, Forest Service, Intermountain Forest and Range Experiment Station. September 1981: 14-16.

Grazing studies began on the Desert Experimental Range during the winter of 1934-1935. Twenty large (129 ha) range pastures were each assigned a season or combination of seasons to be grazed by sheep at different stocking intensities. The rest of the area was divided into 14 units. Over the years, 11 have been grazed by sheep and two by cattle. One unit has not been grazed. It was from studies on these plots that research has shown that proper resource management techniques have the ability to increase forage production by 45 percent. Researchers have demonstrated the importance of season and intensity of grazing on salt desert shrub vegetation. Long-term studies on the Desert Experimental Range have shown that the principal perennial species are long-lived and generally suffer little mortality after the second year of establishment. Many of the research programs on the Desert Experimental Range are cooperative efforts. For example, researchers of the Intermountain Forest and Range Experiment Station's Shrub Sciences Laboratory and the Utah Division of Wildlife Resources have recently completed studies that show antelope can flourish on valley bottoms, where they are not ordinarily found, if drinking water is made available for them.

11. Beale, Donald M.; Scotter, George W. 1968. Seasonal forage use by pronghorn antelope in western Utah. Utah Science 29(1): 3-6, 16.

The general diet of antelope under good forage conditions consist mostly of succulent grasses and forbs during the early spring, mostly succulent forbs during the late spring and summer, forbs and browse in the fall, and browse during the winter. In years when precipitation is low, antelope are forced to take less desirable forage and to utilize less of the succulent forbs and more browse. If the drought is severe, even the quality of browse is reduced. At the Desert Experimental Range *Artemisia nova* provides up to 85 percent of the forage consumed by antelope during much of the winter. Many factors are involved in the ecological relationships of antelope to their range.

12. Beale, Donald M.; Smith, Arthur D. 1967. Immobilization of pronghorn antelopes with succinylcholine chloride. Journal of Wildlife Management 31(4): 840-842.

Succinylcholine chloride was administered intramuscularly by Cap-Chur gun to eight pronghorn antelope (*Antilocapra americana*). The animals were confined to a 40-acre enclosure on the Desert Experimental Range, which permitted repeated dosages on some animals. Effective doses ranged from 6.05 – 9.93 mg/100 lbs of body weight. No mortality resulted and no complications were observed. The drug seems an effective immobilant for this species.

13. Beale, Donald M.; Smith, Arthur D. 1970. Forage use, water consumption, and productivity of pronghorn antelope in western Utah. Journal of Wildlife Management 34(3): 570-582.

USDA Forest Service Gen. Tech. Rep. RMRS-GTR-312WWW. 2013

7

A study of herbage production, forage use, water consumption, and productivity of pronghorn antelope was conducted from 1961 through 1969 on semi-desert range of the Desert Experimental Range in western Utah. Most of the data were obtained from a small herd of antelope confined by a fence to 10,000 acres. Herbage production on the study area ranged from 114-321 lbs. of air-dried herbage per acre over a 5-year period. During the same period, annual precipitation ranged from 4.24-11.13 inches. During summers of above-average rainfall, forbs provided over 90 percent of the diet at the peak of their production. Conversely, in years of below-average summer rainfall, forbs were often scarce and contributed less than 20 percent, browse making up the remainder. Grass was commonly utilized by antelope in early spring and occasionally in late summer and fall if new growth appeared. Succulence appeared to be the major characteristic of the forage sought by the antelope. During late fall and winter when nearly all forbs were dry, their diet was over 90 percent browse, mostly black sagebrush. Antelope water consumption varied inversely with the quantity and succulence of preferred forage species. When forbs were abundant and their moisture content was 75 percent or more, the antelope did not drink water even though it was readily available. As vegetation lost succulence, water consumption began, reaching 3 quarts of water per animal per day during extremely dry periods. Fawn:doe ratios on the study area ranged from 100:100 to 181:100. These ratios are for mature does. A statistical analysis of fawn production to precipitation received during the previous summer months indicated a significant relationship and gave statistical values of $t = 4.42$ (P < 0.01); $r = 0.722$ P <0.05).

14. Beale, Donald M.; Smith, Arthur D. 1973. Mortality of pronghorn antelope fawns in western Utah. Journal of Wildlife Management 37(3): 343-352.

Over a period of 5 years, 117 pronghorn antelope fawns 1-5 days of age were captured in a 4,000-hectare enclosure on the Desert Experimental Range and fitted with radio transmitters to provide a means of relocating them to determine causes of mortality. Each fawn was located and observed daily until approximately 4 months of age or until death. Fawns with transmitters that functioned beyond this period were thereafter checked periodically. A total of 55 cases of fawn mortality were discovered during the study. Bobcats accounted for 27 deaths; golden eagles one; and coyotes one. Two died from salmonellosis, three from pneumonia, four from starvation, and one from an esophageal injury. Eleven were abandoned by does as a result of handling, five of which died. The ages of fawns definitely killed by bobcats ranged from 3 to 104 days; one weighed 22 kg at the time of kill.

USDA Forest Service Gen. Tech. Rep. RMRS-GTR-312WWW. 2013

8

15. Behan, Barbara; Welch, Bruce L. 1985. Black sagebrush: mule deer winter preference and monoterpenoid content. Journal of Range Management 38(3): 278-280.

Wintering mule deer (*Odocoileus hemionus hemionus*) preference was determined for seven accessions of black sagebrush *(Artemisia nova)* grown on a common garden. Preference as expressed as percentage of current annual growth eaten varied from 0.0 to 82.7%. An accession called Pine Valley Ridge from the Desert Experimental Range was significantly preferred by the deer over the other six accessions. No significant relationship was found between monoterpenoid content and preference by mule deer.

16. Blaisdell, James P.; Holmgren, Ralph H. 1984. *Managing intermountain rangelands: salt-desert shrub ranges.* Gen. Tech. Rep. 163. Ogden, UT: U.S. Department of Agriculture, Forest Service, Intermountain Forest and Range Experiment Station. 52 p.

This guide for range managers and users is a distillation of the most important research findings over the past 50 years. The research provides a strong scientific basis for planning and decision making in the management of the salt-desert shrub rangelands of the Great Basin and Intermountain areas, which cover some 40 million acres. Much of research took place in the USDA Forest Service's Desert Experimental Range in southwestern Utah.

17. Bleak, A. T.; Frischkecht, N. C.; Plummer, A. Perry; Eckert, R. E., Jr. 1965. Problems in artificial and natural revegetation of the arid shadscale vegetation zone of Utah and Nevada. Journal of Range Management 18(2): 59-65.

Vast areas of the arid shadscale zone have been rehabilitated through management change, but direct plantings of both native and introduced species usually have failed. Future success will likely be with native plants, including shrubs, adapted to the particular site. Observations and research results from the Desert Experimental Range contributed to the conclusions drawn in this report.

18. Bradford, David F.; Franson, Susan E.; Neale, Anne C; Heggem, Daniel T.; Miller, Glenn R; Canterbury, Grant E. 1998. Bird species assemblages as indicators of biological integrity in Great Basin Rangeland. Environmental Monitoring and Assessment 49: 1-22.

The study evaluates the potential for bird species assemblages to serve as indicators of biological integrity of rangelands in the Great Basin in much the same way that fish and invertebrate assemblages have been used as indicators in aquatic environments. The study approach was to identify metrics of the bird community using relatively simple sampling methods that reflect the degree of rangeland degradation and are consistent over a variety of vegetation types and geographic areas. The study was conducted in three range types (i.e., potential natural plant community types) in each of two widely separated areas of the Great Basin: south-eastern Idaho (sagebrush steppe range types) and west-central Utah on the Desert Experimental

Range (salt-desert shrub range types). Sites were selected in each range type to represent three levels of grazing impact, and in Idaho included sites modified for crested wheatgrass production. Birds were sampled by point counts on nine, 100-m radius plots at 250-m spacing on each of 20 sites in each area during the breeding season. In sagebrush-steppe, 964 individuals in 8 species of passerine birds were used in analysis. Five metrics were significantly related to impact class, both when analyzed within range type and when analyzed with all range types combined. Species richness, relative abundance of shrub obligate species, and relative abundance of Brewer's sparrow were generally lower for the higher impact classes, whereas the reverse was true for dominance by a single species and for relative abundance of horned larks. In contrast, total number of individuals did not differ significantly as a function of impact class. In salt-desert shrub, a total of 843 birds in 4 species were included in analyses, 98% of which were horned larks. None of the metrics identified above was significantly related to impact class. Two metrics for breeding birds in sagebrush steppe (species richness and dominance) showed little overlap between values for the extremes of impact class, and thus they have potential as indicators of biological integrity. However, the sensitivity of these metrics appears to be greatest at the high impact end of the spectrum, which suggests they may have limited utility in distinguishing between sites having light and moderate impact.

19. Brewster, Sam F., Jr. 1968. A study on the effectiveness of precipitation in the salt desert shrub type. Provo, UT: Brigham Young University. 66 p. Thesis.

A study of the effectiveness of precipitation in the Salt Desert Shrub Type was conducted at the Desert Experimental Range in southwestern Millard County, Utah. Effectiveness of precipitation refers to the degree to which precipitation supplies water that is taken into the plant-system. The purpose of this study was to measure quantitatively the effectiveness of precipitation by determining the amount and timing of plant absorption of moisture during the summers of 1965 and 1966. In addition, the effectiveness of precipitation was related to some causal factors; especially those factors that help provide a procedure for calculation of this effectiveness. The effectiveness of moisture resulting from rain storms was extremely variable, ranging from no effective moisture to more than 90 percent of total precipitation. In general, the deeper the rains penetrated into the soil the greater was the effectiveness of the moisture. The effectiveness of a rain event depended upon the amount of water that penetrated below 7 inches and upon the rate of evaporation of available moisture in the soil between the drying front and the 7-inch level. A study of moisture contents of species during the dry summer of 1966 showed that winterfat absorbed more water as the available moisture became exhausted than did shadscale or Indian ricegrass. Thus winterfat appears to be able to make more effective use of limited moisture in the summer and thereby remain in better physiological condition to absorb moisture from subsequent rains.

USDA Forest Service Gen. Tech. Rep. RMRS-GTR-312WWW. 2013

10

20. Chambers, Jeanne Cecile. 1979. The effects of grazing on salt desert shrub species survival during a period of below-average precipitation. Logan, UT: Utah State University. 113 p. Thesis.

It has often been assumed that the negative effects of grazing increase during drought periods. Few studies, however, have actually tested this assumption. One of the most precise methods of assessing community change is through the use of demographic parameters. This study used demographic parameters to determine the combined and separate effects of drought and winter sheep grazing and the relationship of both to vegetation type for perennial salt desert grass and shrub species on the U.S. Forest Service, Desert Experimental Range in southwestern Utah during the 2-year drought period from August 1975 to August 1977. Precipitation during the first 12-month period was 55 percent of the yearly average of 156.9 mm and 70 percent of the average during the second 12-month period. The data set was derived from cover maps and consisted of 1975 and 1977 total densities and all deaths and new introductions that had occurred during the intervening period for 64 non-grazed plots (9.4 m^2) and 76 plots grazed lightly or heavily in the spring or winter. Differences in population changes between grazing treatments and vegetation types during the drought were determined from statistical comparisons of natality and mortality. The response of the shrub species to the effects of drought alone was found by comparing long-term values of natality, mortality, and net population turnover with those obtained for the drought period. The grass species were more susceptible to the detrimental effects of grazing than the shrub species. Heavy spring grazing resulted in high mortalities and low natalities of *Oryzopsis hymenoides*, a cool-season grass, and of *Sporobolus cryptandrus*, a warm-season grass possibly because of increased use by sheep during the drought or because of an inherent susceptibility to drought. Spring grazing increased shrub mortality in general while winter grazing decreased mortality. Survival of the dominant shrub, *Ceratoides lanata*, was benefitted by light winter grazing. Heavy spring grazing resulted in high natalities of *Atriplex confertifolia,* an increaser shrub, and was beneficial to its survival. No significant differences between grazing treatment for *Artemisia spinescens*, a decreaser species, were found and drought appeared to "suspend" the detrimental effects of grazing. Natality and mortality of all species were closely related to vegetation type and it appeared that droughts may have an important role in determining (maintaining) plant community distribution patterns in salt deserts. Natality and mortality of the grass species were more directly correlated to vegetation type than the shrub species. Mortality of *Oryzopsis hymenoides* was higher in shrubby plots; natality of *Sporobolus cryptandrus* was higher in grassy plots. Natality of the shrub species was, in general, highest in shrubby plots. Comparisons of the long-term averages of natality, mortality, and net population turnover of the three shrubby species with those obtained during the drought period showed that drought decreased the rate of population change for all three species regardless of past population trends or responses to grazing. The timing of precipitation during the drought period may have influenced species survival depending upon the phenology of the individual species. Larger population changes may occur during droughts of longer duration and greater severity.

21. Chambers, Jeanne C.; Norton, Brien E. 1993. Effects of grazing and drought on population dynamics of salt desert shrub species on the Desert Experimental Range, Utah. Journal of Arid Environments 24(3): 261-275.

Natality, mortality, and population turnover of dominant salt desert shrub species under different seasons (winter vs. spring) and intensities (light vs. heavy) grazing by domestic sheep during a drought period on the USDA Forest Service Desert Experimental Range in southwestern Utah were examined for this study. Species responses were more predictable from their life history and physiological traits than from past responses to grazing alone. Heavy or spring grazing increased mortality of *Artemisia spinescens*, a cool-season shrub susceptible to past grazing, and of *Sporobolus cryptandrus* and *Atriplex confertifolia*, a C_4 grass and shrub, respectively, that had increased under this grazing regime in the past. Light or winter grazing during this period increased survival and natality of *S. cryptandrus*, and of *Ceratoides lanata*, a shrub that had decreased in density but increased in cover under past grazing. Population turnover rates were generally positive for *A. spinescens*, but were highly negative for *A. confertifolia* in all but the heavy spring grazing treatment. *A. confertifolia* had exhibited high mortality during past droughts. *C. lanata* exhibited little population change reflecting past trends. Generally positive rates of turnover for the two grasses, *S. cryptandrus* and *O. hymenoides,* paralleled past trends, except in the spring-heavy treatment that had highly negative turnover rates. In a comparison of grass vs. shrub dominated vegetation types, *C. lanata* had higher mortality in grass dominated plots; *O. hymenoides* had higher mortality in shrub dominated plots. Both *S. cryptandrus* and *O. hymenoides* exhibited low or negative turnover rates for grazed plots within the shrub dominated type. Overall, light to moderate grazing and the removal of livestock before active physiological growth of cool season species had the least negative effects on population dynamics during a 2-year drought period. This grazing regime increased survival or natality of certain species.

22. Clary, Warren P. 1986. Black sagebrush response to grazing in the east-central Great Basin. In: McArthur, E. Durant; Welch, Bruce L., comps. Proceedings—symposium on the biology of *Artemisia* and *Chrysothamnus*; 1984 July 9-13; Provo, UT. Gen. Tech. Rep. INT-200. Ogden, UT: U.S. Department of Agriculture, Forest Service, Intermountain Research Station: 181-185.

Results from a variety of sites in the Great Basin including the Desert Experimental Range with different sheep or cattle grazing histories show a rather consistent reduction in black sagebrush cover compared to areas that were not grazed. Low-elevation black sagebrush experienced the greatest cover reduction. Moderate use during midwinter or alternate year use during midwinter appears to be compatible with maintaining black sagebrush cover.

USDA Forest Service Gen. Tech. Rep. RMRS-GTR-312WWW. 2013

12

23. Clary, Warren P. 1986. Fifty-year response to grazing in the low-shrub cold desert of the Great Basin, U.S.A. In: Joss, P. J.; Lynch, P. W; Williams, O. B., eds. Rangelands: a resource under siege. Proceedings of the second International Rangeland Congress; 1984, May 13-18; Adelaide, Australia. Canberra, Australia: Australian Academy of Science: 37-38.

A question has arisen concerning the effect of livestock grazing on low-shrub cold desert winter ranges—particularly in the nearly 50 years following a reduction in peak grazing use. This study, conducted in part at the Desert Experimental Range, shows that different plant communities have developed since the 1930s under typical grazed and ungrazed conditions.

24. Clary, Warren P.; Beale, Donald M. 1983. Pronghorn reactions to winter sheep grazing, plant communities, and topography in the Great Basin. Journal of Range Management 36(6): 749-752.

The winter distribution of pronghorn over a 142-km^2 area on the Desert Experimental Range was significantly related to sheep grazing during the current winter, presence of black sagebrush, and topographic characteristics. Even moderate sheep use during the dormant period left grazing units relatively unfavorable for pronghorn until spring regrowth—at least on ranges where key pronghorn forage plants were in short supply. Winter use areas preferred by pronghorn were above the valley bottoms in rolling to broken topography where black sagebrush communities were evident. Movement characteristics of pronghorn have allowed many of them to readily locate to rested grazing units, and, therefore, avoid severe dietary competition with sheep.

25. Clary, Warren P.; Beale, Donald M.; Holmgren, Ralph C. 1985. Melanistic pronghorn fawns on the Desert Experimental Range, Utah. Southwestern Naturalist 30(1): 159-161.

This report documents three occurrences of melanistic pronghorn (*Antilocarpra americana*) fawns born on the Desert Experimental Range in western Utah. Neither personal communications with experienced observers of pronghorns nor the literature has yielded mention of other occurrences of melanistic pronghorn fawns.

26. Clary, Warren P.; Holmgren, Ralph C. 1982. Desert Experimental Range: establishment and research contribution. *Rangelands* 4:261–264.

The Desert Experimental Range in southwestern Utah is typical of winter grazing lands in the Great Basin and parts of adjacent physiographic provinces. These arid lands are low-shrub desert that have been variously designated the shadscale association, the northern desert shrub formation, or the salt-desert shrub association. Climatically, the country is a cold desert; cold winters, warm summers. This low-shrub desert has been used as a winter range since the late 19th century soon after domestic livestock arrived in the Intermountain West. The experimental range was established when President Herbert Hoover withdrew 87 square miles of land from the public domain in southwestern Utah as an "agricultural range experiment station" in February 1933. Grazing studies were begun in the winter of 1934-1935. About 75% of the DER is alluvial slope or flat valley bottom bounded by some hills and mountain land. Elevation ranges from 5,075 to 8,415 feet. The soils are mostly gravelly loams, sandy loams, or loamy sands with low clay content (Aridisols and Entisols). Long term temperature extremes have varied from 104 to −40 °F. The DER research has included range management and plant ecology, development of vegetation sampling techniques, and wildlife biology.

27. Clary, Warren P.; Holmgren, Ralph C. 1982. Observations of pronghorn distribution in relation to sheep grazing on the Desert Experimental Range. In: Nelson, Lewis, Jr.; Peek, James, Co-chairmen. Proceedings of the wildlife – livestock relationships symposium; 1981 April 20-22; Coeur d'Alene, ID. Moscow, ID: University of Idaho, Forest, Wildlife & Range Experiment Station: 581-592.

Moderate sheep use during the dormant winter period left grazing units relatively unfavorable for pronghorn until spring plant regrowth occurred. Expanding pronghorn populations on the Desert Experimental Range suggest that if the grazing system used leaves sufficient rested area each winter, sheep use is not greatly limiting to pronghorn populations.

28. Clary, Warren P.; Holmgren, Ralph C. 1987. Difficulties in interpretation of long-term vegetation trends in response to livestock grazing. In: Provenza, Frederick D.; Flinders, Jerran T.; McArthur, E. Durant, comps. Proceedings— symposium on plant-herbivore interactions: 1985 August 7-9; Snowbird, UT. Gen. Tech. Rep. INT-222, Ogden, UT: U.S. Department of Agriculture, Forest Service, Intermountain Research Station: 154-161.

Grazing effects data from the Desert Experimental Range, Utah, are used to illustrate the problems of interpreting vegetation response to grazing treatment, precipitation, and site. Differences in results and analysis may be related to experience, viewpoint, plot sampling, and failure to note climatic patterns, soils, and vegetation cycles.

29. Clary, Warren P.; Holmgren, Ralph H. 1987. Reversal of desertification on the low-shrub desert. In: Aldon, E. F.; Gonzales, V.; Carlors, E.; Moir, W. H., tech. eds. Strategies for classification and management of native vegetation for food production in arid zones; 1987 October 12-16. Gen. Tech. Rep. RM-150. Fort Collins, CO: U.S. Department of Agriculture, Forest Service, Rocky Mountain Forest and Range Experiment Station: 138-142.

The low-shrub cold desert has been used as livestock winter range since the late 19th century. Severe deterioration resulted from earlier, improper grazing practices. Data and observations in the 1970s and 1980s, in part from the Desert Experimental Range, suggest a reversal of desertification has occurred under improved grazing practices.

30. De Soyza, Amrita G.; Van Zee, Justin W.; Whitford, Walter G.; Nealè, Anne; Tallent-Hallsel, Nita; Herrick, Jeffrey E.; Havstad, Kris M. 2000. Indicators of Great Basin rangeland health. Journal of Arid Environments 45(4): 289-304.

Early-warning indicators of rangeland health can be used to estimate the functional integrity of a site and may allow sustainable management of desert rangelands. The utility of several vegetation canopy-based indicators of rangeland health at 32 Great Basin rangeland locations was investigated. The indicators were originally developed in rangelands of the Chihuahuan Desert. Soil resources are lost through wind and water-driven erosion mainly from areas unprotected by plant canopies (i.e. bare soil). Study sites in Idaho had the smallest bare patches, followed by sites in Oregon. The more arid great Basin Sagebrush Zone sites in Utah had the largest bare patches. Several vegetational indicators including percent cover by vegetation, percent cover by life-form, percent cover by sagebrush, and percent cover by resilient species were negatively related to mean bare patch size and are potential indicators of Great Basin rangeland condition. Plant community composition and the range of bare patch sizes were different at sites in the three locations in Idaho, Oregon, and Utah, including the Desert Experimental Range. Therefore, expected indicator values are location specific and should not be extrapolated to other locations. The condition of study sites were often ranked differently by different indicators. Therefore, the condition of rangeland sites should be evaluated using several indicators.

31. Duda, Jeffrey, J.; Freeman, D. Carl; Emlen, John M.; Belnap, Jayne; Kitchen, Stanley G.; Zak, John C.; Sobek, Edward; Tracy, Mary; Montante, James. 2003. Differences in native soil ecology associated with invasion of the exotic annual chenopod, *Halogeton glomeratus*. Biology and Fertility of Soils 38 (2): 72-77.

Various biotic and abiotic components of soil ecology differed significantly across an area on the Desert Experimental Range where *Halogeton glomeratus* is invading a native winterfat, [*Krascheninnikovia (=Ceratoides) lanata*] community. Nutrient levels were significantly different among the native, ecotone, and exotic-derived soils. NO_3, P, K, and Na all increased as the cover of halogeton increased. Only Ca was highest in the winterfat area. A principal components analysis, conducted separately for water-soluble and exchangeable cations, revealed clear separation between halogeton- and winterfat-derived soils. The diversity of soil bacteria was highest in the exotic, intermediate in the ecotone, and lowest in the native community. Although further studies are necessary, our results offer evidence that invasion by halogeton alters soil chemistry and soil ecology, possibly creating conditions that favor halogeton over native plants.

32. Ellison, Lincoln. 1960. Influence of grazing on plant succession of rangelands. Botanical Review 26(1): 1-78.

Succession is commonly thought of as a constructive process: the origins of the word suggest growth and progress. In primary succession the development of soil with its contained organisms, including the complex vegetation it supports, is certainly a constructive process. Most of the familiar forms of secondary succession are also constructive in character. In contrast, secondary successions resulting from grazing are commonly thought of as being other than constructive. There are enough examples of severe overgrazing of range vegetation so that it is generally known that reduction of plant cover by overgrazing leads to accelerated soil erosion by wind or water. Even if grazing changes the character of the vegetation without reducing cover sufficiently to cause erosion, the change is usually toward a vegetation that is less palatable to the grazing animal and somewhat less productive. Various benefits conferred by grazing animals on vegetation have been suggested: (1) cropping may stimulate herbage production; (2) grazing may help a plant endure drought by reducing the area of its transpiring surface; (3) grazing, by removing some of the herbage, lessens the amount of mulch and thus, by encouraging early spring growth, increases production; (4) grazing animals carry the seeds of forage species from place to place; (5) trampling helps plant seeds of forage species; (6) livestock trails check the overland flow of water and thus encourage infiltration; (7) grazing animals fertilize the range. Taken in total, these presumed contributions of grazing animals to the welfare of range vegetation are not impressive. The benefits of grazing, if any, would appear to accrue to the ecosystem, to the range as a whole, instead of to the palatable species of plants that are grazed most. Analyses of data from The Desert and Great Basin Experimental Ranges among other places were drawn on to prepare this review.

33. Franklin, M. A. "Ben." 1996. Field survey for *Sphaeralcea caespitosa* M. E. Jones in the Beaver River and Warm Springs Resource Areas, Beaver and Millard Counties, Utah. Final Report for 1994/1995 Challenge Cost Share Project. Salt Lake City, UT: Utah Department of Natural Resources, Division of Wildlife Resources Utah Natural Heritage Program and USDI Bureau of Land Management Utah State Office. 16 p. + maps and appendices.

Locations of putative *Sphaeralcea caespitosa* populations in the Beaver River and Warm Springs BLM Resource Areas and the Desert Experimental Range were mapped. The numbers of individual plants are sufficiently high and threats insufficient enough to negate the need for the federal listing of the species as a Threatened or Endangered species. However, taxonomic problems need resolution.

34. Freeman, D. Carl; Emlen, John M. 1995. Assessment of interspecific interactions in plant communities: an illustration from the cold desert saltbush grasslands of North America. Journal of Arid Environments 31(2): 179-198.

Interspecific interactions influence both the productivity and composition of plant communities. New field procedures and analytical approaches for assessing interspecific interactions in nature and application of these procedures to the salt desert shrub grasslands of western Utah are proposed. Data were collected from two grazing treatments at the Desert Experimental Range over a period of 2 years. The proposed equations were fairly consistent across both treatments and years. In addition to illustrating how to assess interspecific interactions within a community, a new approach was developed for projecting the community composition as a result of some alteration, i.e. increase or decrease in the abundance of one or more species. Results demonstrate competition both within and between plant life-form groups. While introduced annuals were found to depress profoundly the likelihood of perennial plants replacing themselves, perennials had little influence on annuals. Thus, as native perennials die, they are more likely to be replaced by introduced annuals than for the reverse to occur. Results suggest that unless conditions change, these communities will become increasingly dominated by introduced annuals.

35. Goodrich, Sherel. 1986. Vascular plants of the Desert Experimental Range, Millard County, Utah. Gen. Tech. Rep. INT-209. Ogden, UT: U.S. Department of Agriculture, Forest Service, Intermountain Research Station. 72 p.

Since the establishment of the Desert Experimental Range in 1933, plant specimens have been collected from the area and deposited in the herbarium of the experimental range. These specimens and duplicate specimens have been sent to botanists acquainted with various groups of plants for annotation. From this collection of annotated specimens, a checklist of vascular plants of the area was assembled. This checklist provides the basis for the taxa covered in this flora.

36. Green, Jeffrey S. 1976. Influence of a dry wash habitat on distribution and movement of heteromyid rodents. Provo, UT: Brigham Young University. 26 p. Thesis.

Three heteromyid rodent species were studied in relation to a large dry wash at the Desert Experimental Range in Millard County, Utah, during the summer, 1974. Data were gathered with three trapping grids and analyzed to determine if the dry wash influenced rodent movement and distribution patterns. *Dipodomys ordii* and *D. microps* were distributed non-randomly in the dry wash and adjacent habitat, but *Perognathus longimembris* seemed to be randomly distributed. *Dipodomys ordii* was significantly correlated with wash habitat, but *D. microps* was found most frequently in upland areas. Soil and vegetative differences and competition were possible causes for the observed distribution. The wash was observed as a source of dispersing young *D. ordii*. It was concluded that the dry wash had little effect on daily movement of the rodents observed.

37. Guerra, S. Luis. 1973. The effect of insect damage on Indian ricegrass (*Oryzopsis hymenoides*) in western Utah. Provo, UT: Brigham Young University. 34 p. Thesis.

Indian ricegrass at the Desert Experimental Range 47 miles west of Milford, Utah, is damaged by the larvae of *Coenchroa illibella, Diatrae* sp. and *Typoceris ceraticornis*, the latter being the most destructive. The biology of the insects and the extent of damage inflicted are discussed. Uninfested plants produced more new stems than infested plants. Plants having a basal diameter of 4 to 6.9 cm and 7 to 9.9 cm were the most frequently infested and, consequently, the most severely damaged.

38. Harper, Kimball T. 1959. Vegetational changes in a shadscale-winterfat plant association during twenty-three years of controlled grazing. Provo, UT: Brigham Young University. 68 p. Thesis.

In 1935, studies were commenced at the Desert Experimental Range in Pine Valley, Millard County, Utah, to determine the relative effects of various grazing treatments upon the shadscale [*Atriplex confertifolia* (Torr. & Frem.) S. Wats.] – winterfat [*Eurotia lanata* (Pursh.) Moq.] plant association. Results of this study indicate that distinct vegetational changes have occurred within that plant association during twenty-three years of controlled grazing by sheep. Total plant cover of perennial species upon selected areas of the experimental range was greater in 1958 than in 1935 on all grazed plots as well as on ungrazed plots. Evidence gathered on the public domain indicates that increase in perennial plant cover on grazed areas of the experimental range is largely due to a reduction in grazing pressure since 1935 and not to a more favorable moisture balance in 1958 compared to 1935. Plant cover of shadscale has decreased in relative importance during the period of study on all ungrazed plots and on plots that are not grazed in the spring. Plant cover of winterfat has increased in relative importance on all plots except those that are grazed in the spring. Plant cover of galleta grass has increased in relative importance during the study period on all plots that supported portions of clones of that grass in 1935. Budsage has increased greatly in importance only on ungrazed plots. The relative importance of all other perennial plant species occurring on the plots studied was little different in 1958 from 1935. Individuals of five of the thirteen plant species studied have been observed to survive from 1935 to 1958. The percentage of budsage and winterfat plants that have been observed to survive from 1935 to 1958 under protection from grazing is larger than the percentage survival of shadscale plants on such areas. Percentage survival of budsage and winterfat plants has declined under stress of grazing, but survival of shadscale plants has generally been greatest on grazed areas. Reproduction of certain species studied has been observed to be related to seasonal distribution of precipitation and to the availability of ecological space in the plant community. Under all grazing treatments tested, the amount of plant cover available for grazing purposes has increased, but under heavy, spring grazing, the relative importance of shadscale has increased at the expense of the better forage plants.

39. Harper, Kimball T.; Van Buren, Renée; Kitchen, Stanley, G. 1996. Invasion of alien annuals and ecological consequences in salt desert shrublands of western Utah. In: Barrow, Jerry R.; McArthur E. Durant; Sosebee, Ronald E.; Tausch, Robin J., comps. Proceedings: shrubland ecosystem dynamics in a changing environment: 1995 May 23-25; Las Cruces, NM. Gen. Tech. Rep. INT-GTR-338. Ogden, UT: U.S. Department of Agriculture, Forest Service, Intermountain Research Station: 58-65.

Vegetation plots in experimentally grazed pastures at the Desert Experimental Range in west-central Utah have been mapped periodically since 1935. The pastures have been grazed at the same intensity and in the same season by sheep from 1935 to the present. Records show that *Bromus tectorum* and *Salsola pestifer* were observed on mapped plots in 1958, although the latter species was reported from the range in 1937. *Halogeton glomeratus* appeared first in 1969. All of these species had become common in both grazed and ungrazed plots by 1989, although plant density and vigor of these aliens were reduced on ungrazed sites. Frequency of occurrence of these species has increased steadily since their first appearance. Experimental studies suggest that soils from areas dominated by *Halogeton* and *Salsola* are associated with lower survival of *Ceratoides lanata* seedlings than soils from healthy *Ceratoides* stands.

40. Harper, Kimball T.; Wagstaff, Fred J.; Clary, Warren P. 1990. Shrub mortality over a 54-year period in shadscale desert, west-central Utah. In: McArthur, E. Durant; Romney, Evan M.; Smith, Stanley D.; Tueller, Paul T., comps. Proceedings—symposium on cheatgrass invasion, shrub die-off, and other aspects of shrub biology and management: 1989 April 5-7; Las Vegas, NV. Gen. Tech. Rep. INT-276. Ogden, UT: U.S. Department of Agriculture, Forest Service, Intermountain Research Station: 119-126.

The Forest Service, U.S. Department of Agriculture, has maintained and repeatedly remapped 100-ft^2 plots on the Desert Experimental Range, Millard County, Utah. Forty-six plots are in areas that have received the same grazing treatments throughout the 54-year period. The data demonstrate that mortality rates for budsage, shadscale, and winterfat have been rather similar throughout the period of record. Although mortality rates for the 1975-1989 period were high, rates were maximal for the period 1968-1975. The recent regional shrub dieoff of the 1980s was during the 1975-1989 data collection interval. Budsage and winterfat had similar rates over the entire period (average of 3.7 percent/yr and 3.3 percent/yr, respectively), but rates for shadscale were more variable from period to period and considerably higher (5.7 percent/yr). Grazing treatments usually had no significant effects on mortality rates for shadscale and winterfat, but late-winter/early spring grazing by sheep often significantly raised the mortality rate for budsage. Late-winter grazing reduced plant recruitment rates for budsage, but increased those rates for shadscale. Recruitment rates for winterfat showed no strong correlations with grazing treatment. Divergent grazing treatment effects on mortality and recruitment rates among these shrub species have resulted in progressive compositional changes in the perennial plant cover at the site. Under protection from grazing, both shadscale and winterfat have continually declined, while budsage has increased. Under early and/or midwinter grazing, budsage increased, winterfat retained a more-or-less stable position in the plant cover, and shadscale declined slowly. Late-winter/early spring grazing has favored shadscale at the expense of both budsage and winterfat. Total above-ground vascular plant cover is greatest in grazing exclosures (23.7 percent), and almost equal in early and late-grazed paddocks (19.7 and 20.1 percent, respectively). Shrub density (species ignored) has declined dramatically on plots grazed in late winter throughout the period of study. On such plots, perennial grasses have increased to keep the plant cover at a rather constant value.

41. Holechek, Jerry L.; Thomas, Milton; Molinar, Francisco; Galt, Dee. 1999. Stocking desert rangelands: what we've learned. Rangelands 21(6): 8-12.

Five stocking rate studies from three different locations in the southwestern United States including the Desert Experimental Range have arrived at essentially the same management recommendations. Desert forage plants can sustain about 40 percent use of annual herbage production. Use in the drought years approached 55-60 percent while use in the wet years was near 20-25 percent. The researchers recommended that desert ranges be routinely stocked for about 30-35 percent use of average forage production with some destocking in drought years. All the studies have indicated that conservative grazing is a reliable way to increase forage production and improve vegetation composition on degraded rangelands. The selection of the correct stocking rate is the most important range management decision. Stocking rate selection is a major problem on desert rangelands in the southwestern United States, where forage production can fluctuate 100 percent among years.

42. Holmgren, Ralph C. 1981. The Desert Experimental Range: description history, and program. In: Arid shrublands—Proceedings of the third workshop of the United States/Australia rangelands panel; 1973 26 March-5 April; Tucson, AZ. Washington, DC: U.S. Government Printing Office: 18-22.

The Desert Experimental Range (DER) is typical of about 180,000 km^2 of winter grazing lands in the Great Basin and in parts of the plateau and mountain physiographic provinces to the north and east. These arid lands are a low-shrub desert that has been variously designated as the shadscale association, the northern desert shrub formation, or the salt-desert shrub association. Climatically, the country is a cold desert: cold winters, warm summers. It became winter range in the late 19th century soon after domestic livestock arrived in the Intermountain West. By fortunate circumstance, the desert range complements other ranges in this region that can only be grazed at other seasons than winter because deep snow prevents their use. Consequently, the year-long grazing operation in the Intermountain area is a system of seasonal use determined by the nature of the country. The DER occupies part of a typical Great Basin valley, some hills, and mountainland. The soils are Aridisols and Entisols. They are loams, sandy loams, or loamy sands; most are skeletal. Clay content is low except on the barren playa in the bottom of the valley. The soils have a pH of around 8.0, and the electrical conductivity ranges for less than 1 mmho/cm in the upper 30 to 40 cm of the profile to 10 to 25 mmho/cm at greater depths. The vegetation is a mosaic of low shrubs and shrub-grass types. The dominant shrub species are *Eurotia lanata, Artemisia spinescens, A. nova, Atriplex confertifolia,* and *Chrysothamnus stenophyllus.* Associated with the shrubs on most soils are perennial grass species; the three most common are *Oryzopsis hymenoides, Hilaria jamesii,* and *Sporobolus cryptandrus.* Grazing studies began in 1934 on 20 large fenced range pastures that were each assigned a season or combination of seasons to be grazed by sheep at one of three stocking intensities. Data have been collected continuously since the DER was established with development of research tools and techniques of use at the DER and elsewhere. The DER has also been important in range management, plant ecology, wildlife, small mammal, and range insect studies.

43. Holmgren, Ralph C. 1984. The Great Basin Cold Desert: some physical geography. In: Tiedemann, Arthur R.; McArthur, E. Durant; Stutz, Howard C.; Stevens, Richard; Johnson, Kendall L., comps. Proceedings—symposium on the biology of *Atriplex* and related chenopods; 1983 May 2-6; Provo, UT. Gen. Tech. Rep. INT-172. Ogden, UT: U.S. Department of Agriculture, Forest Service, Intermountain Forest and Range Experiment Station: 108-113.

This paper presents an overview of the geological history, physiography, climate, and hydrology of the eastern Great Basin as background in a discussion of the nomenclature of the major regional desert plant associations of the cold desert of inland western North America including the Desert Experimental Range area.

44. Holmgren, Ralph C.; Brewster, Sam F., Jr. 1972. Distribution of organic matter reserve in a desert shrub community. Res. Pap. INT-130. Ogden, UT: U.S. Department of Agriculture, Forest Service, Intermountain Forest and Range Experiment Station. 15 p.

Of the total accumulated organic mass (about 1,770 g/m^2) in a cold desert shrub community of the Desert Experimental Range in western Utah, 13.5 percent is above the ground. About half the root mass is in the top 30 cm of soil, 30 percent in the second 30 cm, 15 percent in the third 30 cm, 3 percent in the fourth 30 cm, and 1 percent below 120 cm to about 135 cm. Coarse roots are found only under or near plants, fine roots are rather evenly distributed horizontally at all depths; they are most abundant in the 7.5- to 15-cm layer, but few are found in the 6- to 7.5-cm layer.

45. Holmgren, Ralph C.; Hutchings, Selar S. 1972. Salt desert shrub response to grazing use. In: McKell, Cyrus M.; Blaisdell, James P.; Goodin, Joe R., tech. eds. Wildland shrubs—their biology and utilization: an international symposium; 1971 July; Logan, UT. Gen. Tech. Rep. INT-1. Ogden, UT: U.S. Department of Agriculture, Forest Service, Intermountain Forest and Range Experiment Station: 153-164.

The salt desert shrub is a unique range type with a broad expanse in the inland west of the United States. The shrubs *Artemisia nova, A. spinescens,* and *Eurotia lanata* are nutritious and palatable and considered to be desirable browse species. Less desirable shrubs from a grazing perspective are *Atriplex confertifolia* and *Chrysothamnus stenoplyllus.* Important cool season grasses are *Oryzopsis hymenoides, Sitanion hystrix,* and *Poa sandbergii,* and *Hilaria jamesii, Sporobolus cryptandrus,* and *Bouteloua gracilis* are important warm season grasses. The highest and most valuable use of the salt desert is as winter range for livestock. Successional change patterns in the salt desert have been established by monitoring seasonal grazing pressures at the Desert Experimental Range.

46. Hutchings, Selar S. 1946. Drive the water to the sheep. National Wool Grower. 36(4): 10-11, 48.

Hauling water to sheep on western ranges can increase the owner's income. Sheep that get enough water to drink every day are healthier and show greater weight gains than sheep that go thirsty. Data from the Desert Experimental Range show that higher lamb crops, better grazing management, and more efficient use of range forage are additional potential benefits.

47. Hutchings, Selar S. 1950. Forecasting forage on the winter range, 1951. National Wool Grower 4(10): 12, 36.

The amount of range forage during the forthcoming grazing season over the winter range country varies from about average to well below average. Grazing prospects can therefore be said to be only fair for most of the winter range. This is indicated by estimates made at the Desert Experimental Range in western Millard County, Utah. These estimates are based on studies correlating total herbage production on October 1st with the previous 12 months precipitation.

48. Hutchings, Selar S. 1951. Winter range forage forecast. National Wool Grower 41(7): 12.

Late summer rains on many of the winter ranges including the Desert Experimental Range have stimulated growth of a number of forage species. Although the fresh green forage is of good quality, total production will still be inadequate to care for the full number of livestock throughout the winter. Because of the low production over most of the winter range, stockmen will need to provide supplemental feed to augment the range forage and in some cases it may be necessary to feed entire bands during a portion of the winter.

49. Hutchings, Selar S. 1954. Managing winter sheep range for greater profit. U.S. Department of Agriculture Farmers' Bulletin. Washington, DC: U.S. Government Printing Office. 46 p.

Good range management provides for protection and improvement of the soil and plant cover, and utilization of the forage crop, as well as care of the sheep grazing the range. The livestock manager has at his disposal many tools to aid him. Knowledge  of important species, annual measurement of the forage crop, and periodic evaluation of range condition are all essential in applying good management. With this information at his command the land manager can balance grazing with forage, provide for moderate and uniform use of range, eliminate excess trailing, provide adequate water, and have on hand ample supplemental feed for emergency periods. The application of any one of these practices will be beneficial but maximum benefit comes with the careful use of all. Good grazing management is concerned primarily with the maintenance, production, and utilization of desirable forage species. These plants largely control grazing capacity while range condition is evaluated on the basis of association and relative vigor of the desirable and undesirable forage species. Stockmen and range managers therefore should know the important range plants, both desirable and undesirable, their growth requirements, and their forage quality. This report lists many of those plants and their characteristics and is drawn, in part, from experience at the Desert Experimental Range.

50. Hutchings, Selar S. 1958. Hauling water to sheep on western ranges. Leaflet No. 423. Washington, DC: U.S. Department of Agriculture. 8 p.

Hauling water to sheep on western ranges, wherever stock watering places are few and far between, can increase the owner's income. Sheep that get enough water to drink every day without trailing long distances for it are healthier and show greater weight gains than sheep that go thirsty. Lamb crops are higher. Water hauling permits better grazing management and more efficient use of range forage. These conclusions are drawn, in part, from experience at the Desert Experimental Range.

51. Hutchings, S. S. 1966. Grazing management of salt-desert shrub ranges in the western United States. In: Proceedings of the IX International Grassland Congress; 1965; São Paulo, Brazil. São Paulo, Brazil: IX International Grassland Congress: 1619-1625.

USDA Forest Service Gen. Tech. Rep. RMRS-GTR-312WWW. 2013

24

Salt-desert shrub ranges occupy approximately 50 million acres in the western United States and furnish forage for about 5 million sheep and several hundred thousand cattle from October to April. Precipitation on these arid lands averages less than 10 inches annually. Soils are moderately saline, and vegetation is chiefly sparse low shrubs and grasses. During the period of 1880 to 1930, unregulated grazing destroyed or injured many desirable forage species such as *Eurotia lanata*, *Artemisia nova* and *Artemisia spinescens*. Undesirable species—*Salsola kali*, *Chrysothamnus stenophyllus*, and more recently *Halogeton glomeratus*—invaded the depleted ranges. Since 1934, research on intensity and period of grazing has demonstrated that both forage and sheep production can be increased by moderate stocking and controlled grazing. At the Desert Experimental Range maintained by the U.S. Forest Service in western Utah, desirable forage species increased 2 to 9 times on many range areas, and undesirable species decreased.

52. Hutchings, Selar S. 1966. Research needs and basic management considerations on salt-desert ranges. In: Salt Desert Shrub Symposium; 1966 August 1-4; Cedar City, UT. Salt Lake City, UT: Bureau of Land Management: 238-256.

There are vast opportunities for research in the salt-desert shrub zone, especially if the concept of multiple-use is applied. At present, range management is the predominant activity on these lands; consequently most research studies should be on the management and improvement of the ranges for livestock grazing. However, research activities should recognize other uses and be flexible enough to change with economic and social pressures. Observations and research at the Desert Experimental Range were valuable in drawing these conclusions.

53. Hutchings, Selar S.; Holmgren, Ralph C. 1959. Interpretation of loop-frequency data as a measure of plant cover. Ecology 40(4): 668-677.

The inherent positive bias of the loop-frequency index as an index of percent plant area depends on plot (loop) size, and on number and size of plants. Algebraic equations by which loop indices may be converted to percent plant area are given. The influence of plant distribution pattern on the bias is shown, and a way to eliminate this effect, which cannot be corrected by mathematical manipulation, is suggested. Deviation of shape of individual plants from circularity increases the bias, but no formula is available for correcting for this effect. Some of the theoretical relationships were tested on synthetic and natural populations of plants. Results conformed closely to theory. Possible modifications for reducing the inherent bias of the loop-frequency method are discussed. The research leading to this report was conducted, in part, at the Desert Experimental Range.

54. Hutchings, Selar S.; Stewart, George. 1953. Increasing forage yields and sheep production on Intermountain winter ranges. Circular No. 925. Washington, DC: U.S. Department of Agriculture. U.S. Government Printing Office. 63 p.

Winter ranges in the Intermountain region furnish forage for approximately 4 to 5 million sheep for a period of 4 to 6 months. These ranges are extensive, comprising about 65 million acres. They are characterized by low precipitation and scant vegetation. This naturally sparse plant cover has been greatly depleted by grazing overuse from the turn of the century to recent years. The depletion has been further intensified by accelerated wind and water erosion and by droughts. To bring about recovery and ensure maintenance of these important ranges will require knowledge of their grazing potentials and application of improved management practices based on this knowledge. The Desert Experimental Range was established by the Forest Service in 1933 for the study and solution of problems existing on such rangelands. The plant types and subtypes characteristic of the winter range are well represented within the experimental range. Utilization of forage plants was influenced primarily by their level of palatability, but other factors such as relative abundance, stage of maturity, and weather conditions also had considerable influence on the kind of forage eaten. On the basis of findings at the experimental range, condition of winter range areas has been grouped into four broad classes that can be identified by relatively few indicators: good, fair, poor, and very poor. Knowledge of the extent of these condition classes on a range is essential to the application of proper utilization standards and stocking rates. Records obtained at the experimental range indicate that approximately the following proportion of the herbage of major forage species can be eaten during the winter period without impairing their continued productivity: Indian ricegrass 75 percent, black sagebrush 60 percent, winterfat 55 percent, and galleta about 45 percent. To provide for reasonable stability in winter grazing and to assure an adequate forage supply in most years, a basic stocking rate that will utilize 75 percent of average forage production is recommended. Studies at the DER indicate that certain management practices are of benefit to both ranges and sheep.

55. Jorgensen, Clive D.; Smith, H. Duane. 1974. Mini-grids and small mammal estimates. Proceedings of the Utah Academy of Sciences, Arts, and Letters 41(1): 12-18.

Work at the Desert Experimental Range to determine the effect of 37 years of controlled sheep grazing on small mammal distributions and populations was assessed by a system of numerous mini-grids tied to a single base-grid to measure population sizes. This method was designed to obtain comparable data from numerous locations over a vast area, even though all grids could not be trapped simultaneously or with large enough grid designs to provide acceptable confidence if each was considered independent of the base-grid; however, it provides the best large area estimates now available. Since it is a new method, additional work is required to make it as useful as possible and to acquire confidence in the results.

56. Jorgensen, Clive D.; Smith, H. Duane; Garcia, James R. 1980. Temporal activity patterns of a *Dipodomys ordii* population. Great Basin Naturalist 40(3): 282-286.

Temporal activity patterns for *Dimodomys ordii* were generally bimodal during the summer, with the highest peak occurring during early predawn hours when conditions were optimum for water conservation. Removal of dominant members in the population resulted in a substantial shift in the activity pattern to increased activity during the evening hours.

USDA Forest Service Gen. Tech. Rep. RMRS-GTR-312WWW. 2013

26

57. Kitchen, Stanley G.; Carlson, Stephanie L. 2008. Great Basin cold desert shrublands and the Desert Experimental Range. In: Kitchen, Stanley G.; Pendleton, Rosemary L.; Monaco, Thomas A.; Vernon, Jason, comps. Proceedings—shrublands under fire: disturbance and recovery in a changing world; 2006 June 6-8; Cedar City, UT. Proceedings RMRS-P-32. Fort Collins, CO: U.S. Department of Agriculture, Forest Service, Rocky Mountain Research Station: 181-185.

This field trip summary briefly describes the geology, geography, and ecology of the Great Basin and the stops of the field trip. The field trips included (1) pigmy rabbit colony and habitat and big and black sagebrush habitat comparisons, (2) mountain big sagebrush burn site and Utah prairie dog rehabilitation site, (3) Wah Wah Summit—juniper expansion into desert grasslands and shrublands, (4) Desert Experimental Range Headquarters, (5) Desert Experimental Range Research Natural Area including its history, ecology of salt-desert shrublands, ecology of burrow islands within the salt-desert shrublands, and sheep grazing studies, (6) Desert Experimental Range area where halogeton invasion of winterfat shrublands has occurred, (7) the Frisco Mine town site, and (8) the Greenville Bench pinyon-juniper treatment and reseeding site.

58. Kitchen, Stanley G.; Hall, Derek B. 1996. Community stability in a salt-desert shrubland grazed by sheep: the Desert Experimental Range story. In: Barrow, Jerry R.; McArthur E. Durant; Sosebee, Ronald E.; Tausch, Robin J., comps. Proceedings: shrubland ecosystem dynamics in a changing environment; 1995 May 23-25; Las Cruces, NM. Gen. Tech. Rep. INT-GTR-338. Ogden, UT: U.S. Department of Agriculture, Forest Service, Intermountain Research Station: 102-107.

The effects of 59 years of winter and spring grazing on a Great Basin salt-desert shrubland at the Desert Experimental Range were analyzed using frequency and cover data. Spring grazing altered species composition more than winter grazing when compared to the non-grazed exclosures. Grazing in both seasons resulted in significant decreases in shrub importance. Introduced annuals increased in importance with spring grazing. Spring-grazed pastures show patterns of destabilization that are missing from winter-grazed pastures and non-grazed exclosures.

59. Kitchen, Stanley G.; Hall, Derek B. 1996. Diversity and sheep grazing-induced compositional shifts in salt-desert communities (USA). In: Proceedings of the fifth international rangeland congress, Volume 1, Contributed presentations; 1995 July 23-28. Denver, CO: Society for Range Management: 292-293.

The effects of 59 years of controlled sheep grazing and exclusion on a Great Basin salt-desert shrubland (Desert Experimental Range, USA) were investigated. Grazing-related differences in species frequencies occurred for nine prominent species found in 32 sets of paired (grazed and ungrazed) sample areas. Grazing-related differences in species diversity were not significant ($p < 0.10$). Sheep grazing drives compositional shifts creating communities with altered resource values.

60. Kitchen, Stanley G.; Jorgensen, Gary L. 2001. Winterfat decline and halogeton spread in the Great Basin. In: McArthur, E. Durant; Fairbanks, Daniel J., comps. Shrubland ecosystem genetics and biodiversity: Proceedings; 2000 June 13-15; Provo, UT. Proceedings RMRS-P-21. Ogden, UT: U.S. Department of Agriculture, Forest Service, Rocky Mountain Research Station: 200-203.

Winterfat (*Ceratoides lanata*) is a long-lived shrub with excellent drought tolerance and good to moderate tolerance for herbivory. It often occurs as near monocultures in deep fine-textured soils of alluvial fans and valley bottoms. Winterfat communities are second only to those of shadscale (*Atriplex confertifolia*) in dominance of the 16 million ha of salt-desert shrublands found in Western North America. In spite of improved grazing practices, winterfat is declining in many areas of the Great Basin. The Eurasian summer annual, halogeton (*Halogeton glomeratus*), is well adapted to the soils and climate associated with winterfat communities and is invasive, replacing winterfat on degraded sites. Recolonization of halogeton stands by winterfat is rare. Subsequently, distinct winterfat- and halogeton-dominated communities often occur side by side. At the Desert Experimental Range (Utah), episodic winterfat mortality at the ecotone has been observed particularly after flood events and periods of higher than average precipitation. The upward translocation and accumulation of cations, particularly sodium, in the soil by halogeton may account, at least in part, for the lack of winterfat establishment in halogeton stands. Other evidence suggests that a possible halogeton-induced change in soil microbiota may also be unfavorable for winterfat. The development of viable management options to restore winterfat communities will require a greater understanding of plant-soil interactions for these species.

61. Kitchen, Stanley G.; Jorgensen, Gary L. 1999. Annualization of rodent burrow clusters and winterfat decline in a salt-desert community. In: McArthur, E. Durant; Oster, W. Kent; Wambolt, Carl L., comps. Proceedings: shrubland ecotones; 1998 August 12-14; Ephraim, UT. Proceedings RMRS-P-11. Ogden, UT: U.S. Department of Agriculture, Forest Service, Rocky Mountain Research Station: 175-180.

Winterfat (*Ceratoides lanata*) is dominant or co-dominant on much of the 16 million ha of salt-desert shrublands of Western North America. This species is in decline in much of the Great Basin and has been so for 20+ years at the Desert Experimental Range (DER), Pine Valley, Utah. Previously, winterfat dominated vegetation on rodent burrow clusters (RBCs) also known as "silver dollars," landscape features commonly associated with calcareous alluvial soils. Presently Eurasian annuals dominate most RBCs. In this study, mean winterfat density was 3.60 plants/m^2 on

USDA Forest Service Gen. Tech. Rep. RMRS-GTR-312WWW. 2013

28

RBC interspaces and 4.78 plants/m^2 on intact RBCs compared to 0.73 plants/ m^2 on annualized RBCs. Winterfat seed production (viable seed/m^2) on intact RBCs was six-fold that of annualized RBCs and three-fold that of interspaces. To the extent that winterfat stand renewal is seed limited, RBC annualization appears to contribute disproportionately to population decline of winterfat.

62. Kitchen, Stanley G.; McArthur, E. Durant. 1996. Desert Experimental Range. In: Schmidt, Wyman C.; Friede, Judy L.; comps. Experimental forests, ranges, and watersheds in the Northern Rocky Mountains: a compendium of outdoor laboratories in Utah, Idaho, and Montana. Gen. Tech. Rep. INT-GTR-334. Ogden, UT: U.S. Department of Agriculture, Forest Service, Intermountain Research Station: 15-21.

This contribution describes the setting, history, climate, soils, plant communities, data bases (climate, vegetation, maps and photographs, publications), examples of research, facilities, and location of the Desert Experimental Range.

63. Kitchen, Stanley G.; McArthur, E. Durant; Jorgensen, Gary L. 1999. Species richness and community structure along a Great Basin elevational gradient. In: McArthur, E. Durant; Oster, W. Kent; Wambolt, Carl L., comps. Proceedings: shrubland ecotones; 1998 August 12-14; Ephraim, UT. Proceedings RMRS-P-11. Ogden, UT: U.S. Department of Agriculture, Forest Service, Rocky Mountain Research Station: 59-65.

Benchmarks for preservation of biological richness can be established by surveying representative reference areas at multiple spatial and temporal scales. In this study, vascular plant species richness was sampled using nested frequency plots (0.25-64 m^2) at 14 sites along a southeastern Great Basin elevational gradient (1,550-2,675 m). The elevational gradient included a portion of the Desert Experimental Range. Salt-desert shrubland, pinyon/juniper woodland, and mixed coniferous forest communities were represented. Species area curves revealed contrasting distribution patterns for perennial grasses, shrubs, and forbs. Multi-scale nested frequency plots provided an efficient method for surveying species richness in these communities.

64. Klade, Richard J. 2006. Building a research legacy, The Intermountain Station, 1911-1997. Gen. Tech. Rep. RMRS-GTR-184. Fort Collins, CO: U.S. Department of Agriculture, Forest Service, Rocky Mountain Research Station. 259 p.

This publication includes highlights of the history of organizations that preceded formation of the Intermountain Forest and Range Experiment Station in 1954. It provides detailed accounts of Intermountain Station research and administrative accomplishments, some of the people who led activities and changes in the organization from 1954 through 1997 when the Intermountain and Rocky Mountain Stations merged to become the Rocky Mountain Research Station. Many significant Station publications are indicated by title in the text, and the references list includes other publications that provide additional historic background on research programs and results including activities at the Desert Experimental Range.

65. Klade, Richard J. 2006. Chapter 7, The Intermountain Station, 1928-1953. In: Klade, Richard J. 2006. Building a research legacy, The Intermountain Station, 1911-1997. Gen. Tech. Rep. RMRS-GTR-184. Fort Collins, CO: U.S. Department of Agriculture, Forest Service, Rocky Mountain Research Station: 55-74.

This chapter includes the documentation of the establishment of the Desert Experimental Range, including its physical setting, facility development, and the initiation of the longest, continuous, specific grazing study in existence.

66. Klade, Richard J. 2006. Chapter 11, New approaches, 1971-1990. In: Klade, Richard J. 2006. Building a research legacy, The Intermountain Station, 1911-1997. Gen. Tech. Rep. RMRS-GTR-184. Fort Collins, CO: U.S. Department of Agriculture, Forest Service, Rocky Mountain Research Station: 129-206.

This chapter includes a summary of the 50-year sheep grazing study on salt-desert shrubs on winter ranges and shift in research priorities at the Desert Experimental Range to emphasize disturbance and successional processes, rodent ecology, pronghorn biology and management, soil crust ecology, and bird and mammal population dynamics in addition to the continuance of sheep grazing. It also documents the establishment of a Research Natural Area in the DER and inclusion of the DER in the UNESCO Man and Biosphere Program as a Biosphere Reserve making it the only cold-desert Biosphere Reserve in the Western Hemisphere. It also documents the publication of *Managing Intermountain Rangelands—Salt-Desert Ranges* based on 50 years of DER research.

67. Klade, Richard J. 2006. Appendix B, A few days with Ralph at the Desert Range. 2006. In: Klade, Richard J. 2006. Building a research legacy, The Intermountain Station, 1911-1997. Gen. Tech. Rep. RMRS-GTR-184. Fort Collins, CO: U.S. Department of Agriculture, Forest Service, Rocky Mountain Research Station: 250-253.

This appendix recounts Intermountain Research Station Editor Richard Klade's visit to the Desert Experimental Range (DER) in June 1976 ostensibly to help DER manager Ralph Holmgren with some manuscript writing. Instead Klade learned firsthand the operation of the DER, Holmgren's unorthodox but effective management style, and participated in a field tour and ecology workshop with visiting agency personnel.

68. Laycock, W. A. 1969. Exclosures and natural areas on rangelands in Utah. Res. Pap. INT-62. Ogden, UT: U.S. Department of Agriculture, Forest Service, Intermountain Forest and Range Experiment Station. 44 p.

This Research Paper presents a listing of 529 areas in Utah that have received little or no use by domestic livestock. Areas are indexed by county, elevation, date established, vegetation type, and type of animal excluded. Locations are further described by section, township, and range; vegetational information is also given. Exclosures at the Desert Experimental Range are included.

69. Marble, James Russell. 1990. Rangeland microphytic crust management, distribution, grazing impacts, and mineral nutrition relations. Provo, UT: Brigham Young University. 78 p. Dissertation.

The relationship of total and relative cover contributed by microphytic and vascular plants growing on soil surfaces as reported for various sites in Utah, including the Desert Experimental Range, was examined. These parameters were regressed against altitude (adjusted for latitude). The absolute and relative cover contributed by microphytic plants decreases dramatically as altitude increases. The absolute relative cover of vascular plants in the data set considered was the reverse of that shown for microphytic taxa. The observed patterns suggest that microphytic species are more tolerant of extreme arid conditions than vascular species, but that non-vascular taxa cannot compete for light when living vascular plant cover and litter reach high values. The influence of various factors on the distribution and abundance of microphytic soil crusts was summarized. This summary should permit a first approximation concerning where in a landscape microphytic plants might contribute significantly to total plant cover. Managers of sites where microphytes are important components of the protective cover of soils may find that long-term stability of such ecosystems will require maintenance of vigorous microphytic covers on soil surfaces. Cover, species richness, and species sum frequency of vascular and non-vascular components of the plant community were inventoried in experimental grazing pastures at the Desert Experimental Range, Millard County, Utah. Grazing treatments considered have been applied continuously for over 50 years. When various combinations of grazing season and intensity were considered, grazed areas had lower vascular and non-vascular plant cover, species richness values, and lower values for species sum frequency than paired control plots. In relative terms, non-vascular cover was reduced 9.8 percent (standard deviation, S = 2.12) by heavy grazing (relative to controls), but under light grazing the decline was only 52.3 percent (S = 39.14). [It appears that these values may be reversed or otherwise cited incorrectly. They are listed here as printed in the original abstract.] Although seasonal grazing effects (early and/or midwinter versus mid and/or late winter or late winter use alone) do not have a statistically significant impact on soil microphyte cover, the results consistently show any combination of late season grazing to be more damaging to microphyte cover than any combination of use in early and /or midwinter. Heavy intensity and late winter grazing thus reduce the cover of non-vascular plants on soil surfaces. The increase in soil surface coverage should make soils more resistant to wind and water erosion. Microphytic crust dominated by *Collema tenax* (a nitrogen-fixing lichen) was removed or left intact around randomly chosen individuals of *Lepidium montanum* var. *montanum* (Nutt. In T. & G), a biennial or short-lived perennial herb of the Great Basin Desert. Plants were harvested at the fruiting stage to evaluate the effect of the microphyte crust on plant water relations, growth and nutrient content. Stepwise discriminate analysis indicted that plant tissue Fe, Mn, P, and Na were significant discriminators between control and treatment plants. Pairwise t-tests showed significant differences between treatment and control plants for tissue Na and K with control plants containing more of each element. Three additional essential minerals (Ca, Cu, and Mg) approached statistical significance (P < 0.10) between treatment and control plants, again with the elements being in largest relative amounts in control plants. Although differences between plants for other elements essential for plant growth were not statistically different, all of those elements (B, Fe, Mn, Mo, N, P, and Zn) occurred in largest relative amounts in control plants. In combination, these data suggest that the microplant assemblages of soil surfaces exert a significant effect on the mineral nutrient supply of associated vascular plants.

70. Marble, James R.; Harper, Kimball, T. 1989. Effect of timing of grazing on soil-surface crytpogamic communities in a Great Basin low-shrub desert: a preliminary report. Great Basin Naturalist 49(11): 104-107.

Cover and species richness of vascular and cryptogamic components of the plant community were inventoried in experimental grazing paddocks at the USDA/FS Desert Range Experiment Station (Desert Experimental Range), Millard County, Utah. The grazing treatments considered have been applied continuously for over 50 years. The effects of heavy (ca. 17 sheep days/acre) grazing treatment applied in two different seasons (early winter versus a split between early and late winter) differed significantly between seasons. Cryptoganic cover and cryptogamic species richness both showed larger decreases under early-late as opposed to early winter only grazing. Vascular plant cover (relative to controls) was also redused by early-late winter grazing, but not to a significant degree. Late season grazing, likewise, had no significant effect on number of vascular species per transect.

USDA Forest Service Gen. Tech. Rep. RMRS-GTR-312WWW. 2013

32

71. McArthur, E. Durant. 2001. The Shrub Sciences Laboratory at 25 years: retrospective and prospective. In: McArthur, E. Durant; Fairbanks, Daniel J., comps. Shrubland ecosystem genetics and biodiversity: Proceedings; 2000 June 13-15; Provo, UT. Proc. RMRS-P-21. Ogden, UT: U.S. Department of Agriculture, Forest Service, Rocky Mountain Research Station: 3-41.

The Shrub Sciences Laboratory celebrated its 25th anniversary with the symposium documented by these proceedings and a ceremony honoring people instrumental in its establishment: Mr. A. Perry Plummer represented Forest Service Research and Development and Dr. Howard C. Stutz represented Brigham Young University. The laboratory came into being because of the research foundation in Western shrub ecosystems generated by USDA Forest Service researchers and their colleagues and the need to carry on programmatic research in vast western shrublands. Since establishment of the laboratory, dozens of scientists and professionals with technical and clerical support have conducted shrubland ecosystem research and development centered on shrubland ecosystem ecology and experimental range management including the Desert Experimental Range. Research focal areas include winter livestock management on salt shrublands; seed quality testing and production and seed and seedbed ecology and adaptation; genetic variation, population biology, and systematics and taxonomy; breeding systems, hybridization, and hybrid zones; rangeland rehabilitation and restoration; equipment development, and cultural care of wildland species; soil/plant interactions, pathology, entomology, and mycorrhizae; nutritive quality, palatability, and wildlife habitat; and invasive weeds and weed biology. A continuing robust research program is anticipated that will build on previous research accomplishments, and will especially emphasize genetic variation and plant material development, fire susceptible ecosystems, invasive weed control and biology, and the ecology and restoration of ecosystems on the urban/wildland interface. Laboratory personnel and collaborators have published nearly 800 titles during the past quarter century.

72. McArthur, Lawrence B. 1977. Utilization of nest boxes by birds in three vegetational communities with special reference to the American kestrel (*Falco sparverius*). Provo, UT: Brigham Young University. 42 p. Thesis.

This study was designed to determine if, by providing artificial nest sites, a raptorial predator could be attracted into an area where suitable sites are limited. The American kestrel (*Falco sparverius*) was a common species in the area and nest boxes designed for their use were place in three vegetational types in western Utah and eastern Nevada including sites at the Desert Experimental Range. Seventy boxes were available in 1975 and 110 in 1976. Kestrels nested both years in the salt-desert shrub community but were absent from the pinyon-juniper and riparian areas. Four other bird species nested in the latter two areas. In 1975 the nesting success was affected by severe weather including unseasonable cold and snow. In 1976, interaction with and predation by rodents affected utilization and success. Other factors such as existing hole-nesting populations, size, construction, and placement of the box also affect the rate of occupancy and number of boxes used.

73. McGinnies, William J. 1949. Reducing hazards of winter grazing. National Wool Grower 39(10): 14-15, 36.

Grazing on the west desert of Utah has always been hazardous. In 1859, Captain Simpson reported heavy losses in herds of beef cattle that underwent the rigors of the desert winter without shelter or supplementary feed. However, in 1875 the young Mormon pioneers, Israel and David Bennion, took a band of sheep to the Riverbed Desert in west central Utah to spend the winter. Although the boys and sheep suffered severe hardships, the herd survived without undo loss. It was not long until many other sheepmen were trailing their herds into western Utah for winter forage. But every year since then, winter grazing has been a gamble; there may be too much snow, or the forage may be inadequate, or any one of a number of other factors can cause excessive losses. Perhaps the easiest way to keep sheep in good condition during the winter grazing season is to use good range management practices. Sheepmen who did so reported that death losses were reduced because of the better flesh on the sheep. All the practices discussed helped to reduce losses in the herds examined during the survey. The management practices, in part from the Desert Experimental Range, found to be most effective were (1) moderate grazing, (2) water hauling, (3) open herding, (4) close culling in the fall, and (5) shipping to and from the winter range.

74. Monsen, Stephen B.; Stevens, Richard; Shaw, Nancy L., comps. 2004. Restoring western ranges and wildlands. Gen. Tech. Rep. RMRS GTR-136. Fort Collins, CO: U.S. Department of Agriculture, Forest Service, Rocky Mountain Research Station. 3 volumes, 884 p.

This three volume set provides background on philosophy, processes, plant materials selection, site preparation and seed and seeding equipment for revegetating disturbed rangelands, emphasizing use of native species. The conclusions and recommendations were drawn, in part, from research experiences on the Desert Experimental Range. The cover photograph of the three volumes is a composite photograph of a Desert Experimental Range scene.

75. Nelson, David L.; Harper, Kimball T.; Boyer, Kenneth C.; Weber, Darrell, J.; Haws, Austin, Marble, James R. 1989. Wildland shrub dieoffs in Utah: an approach to understanding the cause. In: Wallace, Arthur; McArthur, E. Durant; Haferkamp, Marshall, comps. Proceedings—symposium on shrub ecophysiology and biotechniology; 1987 Jun 30 – July 2, Logan, UT. Gen. Tech. Rep. INT-256. Ogden, UT: U.S. Department of Agriculture, Forest Service, Intermountain Research Station: 119-135.

A survey of the 1984-1885 shrub dieoff in eastern and central Utah showed 734,500 acres of rangeland to be affected. Additional unsurveyed dieoffs occurred in western Utah valleys. Shrub species affected include shadscale, fourwing saltbush, budsage, winterfat, horsebrush, narrowleaf low rabbitbrush, and others. Although earlier dieoffs have been associated with severe drought, the recent dieoff was associated with a record high precipitations period. Possible interacting factors include overgrazing, winter injury, drought, salinity-anaerobiosis, insects, disease, and host genetics. Information from the literature on these factors, the nature of past shrub dieoffs reported, and environmental factors coincident with the recent high precipitation period (1977-1986) are considered in formulating an approach to understanding the cause.

76. Norton, Brien E. 1978. The impact of sheep grazing on long-term successional trends in salt-desert shrub vegetation of southwestern Utah. In: Hyder, Donald. N., ed. Proceedings of the first international rangeland congress; 1978 August 14-18; Denver, CO. Denver, CO: Society for Range Management: 610-613.

Since 1935 the United States Department of Agriculture, Forest Service has conducted a sheep grazing experiment on winter rangeland at the Desert Experimental Range, southwestern Utah. From an initial value of 4 percent in 1935, the cover of perennials in grazed and exclosed vegetation has increased steadily to nearly 9 and 11 percent, respectively. Heavy grazing did not affect the general trend in plant cover or species composition. Under both grazed and protected conditions (1) the least palatable shrub, shadscale, exhibited a short-term rise in total cover followed by a steady decline; and (2) the more palatable co-dominant shrub, winterfat, consistently increased in cover. Contrary to accepted range management theory, the vegetation changes in dominant palatable and unpalatable species were not a function of grazing pressure as mediated by interspecific competition. Inherent plant longevity, opportunity for plant replacement and differential response to climatic pattern may be more influential factors than grazing stress.

77. O'Neal, Gerry Timothy. 1985. Behavioral ecology of the Nevada kit fox (*Vulpes macrotis nevadensis*) on a managed desert rangeland. Provo, UT: Brigham Young University. 76 p. Thesis.

A total of 65 kit foxes were ear tagged at the Desert Experimental Range in western Utah from January to December 1983. Thirty-eight, including adults and juveniles at six den sites, were radio-collared during the course of the study. Mortality rate was 55 percent. Most causes were unknown and may have been related to low body condition indices. Predation by coyotes (*Canis latrans*) was the major known cause of death. Home ranges averaged 2.3 km^2 for males and 1.8 km^2 for females. A negative correlation existed between home range size and body condition indices. A strong dependency on young black-tailed jackrabbits (*Lepus californicus*), Ord's kangaroo rats (*Dipodomys ordii*) and horned larks (*Eremophilia alpestris*) was observed for both adult and young. An expanded social structure was observed as indicated by frequent visitations between foxes from different dens and poor expression of territoriality. Kit foxes did not appear to react to the presence or absence of sheep or cattle. Juveniles began dispersing in mid-August with straight-line distances ranging from 24 to 64 km.

78. O'Neal, G. Timothy; Flinders, Jerran T.; Clary, Warren, P. 1987. Behavioral ecology of the Nevada kit fox (*Vulpes macrotis nevadensis*) on a managed desert rangeland. In: Genoways, Hugh H., ed. New York, NY: Plenum Publishing Corporation. Current Mammalogy 1: 443-481.

Habitat selection, reproduction, food habits, dispersal, and other behavioral expressions of kit foxes on a managed desert rangeland were investigated from January 1983 through December 1983 at the Desert Experimental Range in western Utah. Six adult kit fox pairs along with a juvenile helper from six natal dens were captured and equipped with radio transmitters to document daily and seasonal movements. Twenty-nine male and female pups representing each of the six dens were captured on a weekly basis to determine condition, and a male and female pup from each den were radio collared in midsummer to document daily movements and, later, dispersal. Coyote predation was the largest known cause of death in juveniles. The 1:1 sex ratio of pups and the presence of lactating females suggest that a fairly stable kit fox population occupied the study area. There was a negative correlation between an index of body condition and home range size of adult male kit foxes. Home ranges averaged 3.7 km^2 for males and 3.0 km^2 for females. Diets of both adults and pups appeared unique in that a dependence on a single species was not shown. Straight-line dispersal distances were large, up to 64 km. An influx of immigrants to the study site was observed during and after the resident juveniles had begun dispersing. And expanded social system appears to exist among these kit foxes. Kit foxes did not react to the presence or absence of sheep or cattle, even when these animals were in close proximity to dens or established hunting areas.

79. Pickford, G. D.; Stewart, George. 1935. Coordinate methods of mapping low shrubs. Ecology 16(2): 257-261.

A large number of plots selected at random to eliminate the personal factor in plot selection and to assure obtaining data that are representative of the area being studied are now recognized as essential in studying plant populations. Although one or two carefully selected plots representing average conditions on an area several hundred times the size of the plot will afford some measure of conditions; a larger number of smaller sized plots selected at random will give much more reliable data. The larger number of plots also is better suited to statistical analysis and necessitates a rapid and reasonably accurate system of mapping and summarizing the data. To meet this need in the study of shrubby vegetation, a method of charting the location and perimeter of crowns of low shrubs has been developed in connection with investigations made on sagebrush-wheatgrass and desert shrub ranges (Desert Experimental Range) by the Intermountain Forest and Range Experiment Station. This new manner of charting, termed the coordinate method, has many distinct advantages over methods previously used and may be useful in mapping the undercover on silvicultural plots as well as in range studies.

80. Plummer, A. Perry. 1966. Experience in improving salt desert shrub range by artificial plantings. In: Salt Desert Shrub Symposium; 1966 August 1-4; Cedar City, UT. Salt Lake City, UT: Bureau of Land Management: 130-146.

This report summarizes experiences, approaches, and plant materials for improving salt desert shrub ranges by seeding. Some of these efforts were at the Desert Experimental Range. Areas with less than 8 inches of annual precipitation have not been successfully seeded. Those with above 8 inches annual precipitation might be successfully treated but new approaches including genetic analyses and hybridization should be employed. Sixty-eight species including 33 shrubs, 26 grasses, 9 forbs are listed as warranting thorough investigation for enhancing salt desert shrub ranges.

81. Ponce-Campos, Guillermo E. ; Moran, M. Susan; Huete, Alfredo; Zhang, Yongguang; Bresloff, Cynthia; Huxman, Travis E.; Eamus, Derek; Bosch, David D.; Buda, Anthony R.; Gunter, Stacey A.; Scalley, Tamara Heartsill; Kitchen, Stanley G.; McClaran, Mitchel P.; McNab, W. Henry; Montoya, Diane S.; Morgan, Jack A.; Peters, Debra P. C.; Sadler, E. John. 2013. Ecosystem resilience despite large-scale altered hydroclimatic conditions. Nature 494: 349-352.

Climate change is predicted to increase both drought frequency and duration, and when coupled with substantial warming, will establish a new hydroclimatological model for many regions. Large-scale, warm droughts have recently occurred in North America, Africa, Europe, Amazonia, and Australia, resulting in major effects on terrestrial ecosystems, carbon balance, and food security. In this analysis, the functional response of above-ground net primary production is compared to contrasting hydroclimatic periods in the late twentieth century (1975–1998), and drier, warmer conditions in the early twenty-first century (2000–2009) in the Northern and Southern Hemispheres. A common ecosystem water-use efficiency (WUEe: above-ground net primary production/evapotranspiration) was found across biomes ranging from grassland to forest that indicates an intrinsic system sensitivity to water availability across rainfall regimes, regardless of hydroclimatic conditions. Findings included higher WUEe in drier years that increased significantly with drought to a maximum WUEe across all biomes; and a minimum native state in wetter years that was common across hydroclimatic periods. This indicates biome-scale resilience to the interannual variability associated with the early twenty-first century drought—that is, the capacity to tolerate low, annual precipitation and to respond to subsequent periods of favorable water balance. These findings provide a conceptual model of ecosystem properties at the decadal scale applicable to the widespread altered hydroclimatic conditions that are predicted for later this century. Understanding the hydroclimatic threshold that will break down ecosystem resilience and alter maximum WUEe may allow prediction of land-surface consequences as large regions become more arid, starting with water-limited, low-productivity grasslands. The Desert Experimental Range was one of a network of 29 sites used in this analysis.

82. Robinove, Charles J.; Chavez, Pat S., Jr.; Gehring, Dale; Holmgren, Ralph. 1981. Arid land monitoring using Landsat albedo difference images. Remote Sensing of Environment 11: 133-156.

The Landsat albedo, or percentage of incoming radiation reflected from the ground in the wavelength range of 0.5 μm to 1.1 μm, is calculated from an equation using the Landsat digital brightness values and solar irradiance values, and correcting for atmospheric scattering, multispectral scanner calibration, and sun angle. The albedo calculated for each pixel is used to create an albedo image, whose grey scale is proportional to the albedo. Differencing sequential registered images and mapping selected values of the difference is used to create quantitative maps of increased or decreased albedo values of the terrain. All maps and other output products are in black and white rather than color, thus making the method quite economical. Decreases of albedo in arid regions may indicate improvement of land quality; increases may indicate degradation. Tests of the albedo difference mapping method in the Desert Experimental Range in southwestern Utah (a cold desert with little long-term terrain change) for a 4-year period show that mapped changes can be correlated with erosion from flash floods, increased or decreased soil moisture, and increases or decreases in the density of desert vegetation, both perennial shrubs and annual plants. All terrain changes identified in this test were related to variations in precipitation. Although further tests of this method in hot deserts showing severe "desertification" are needed, the method is nevertheless recommended for experimental use in monitoring terrain change in other arid and semiarid regions of the world.

83. Shandruck, L. J. 1975. A comparison of three methods used to analyze pronghorn antelope diets. Logan, UT: Utah State University. 118 p. Thesis.

An increasing interest in fecal analysis as a method of determining diets of herbivores prompted research to determine if this method could be used successfully to determine diets of pronghorn antelope found in Utah's cold desert rangelands. In addition to fecal analysis, quantitative estimates of pronghorn diets were derived from rumen analysis and feeding site observations. Rumen samples were analyzed by three different methods: (1) microscopic, (2) gravimetric, and (3) point frame. In addition to field experiments, samples from a feeding trial with a diet of known composition were used to determine whether or not differential digestion of plant epidermis occurs. Fourteen male pronghorn antelope were collected between July 1970 and June 4, 1971, on the Desert Experimental Range near Milford, Utah. A fecal sample was taken from the intestine of each. In addition, fecal samples and estimates of vegetative composition were collected at 14 sites. These, plus eight

USDA Forest Service Gen. Tech. Rep. RMRS-GTR-312WWW. 2013

38

rumen samples collected from hunter kills during August 1970 were used to compare methods of rumen analysis and fecal analysis with the other conventional techniques used in this study. Of the methods used, the microscopic technique, as described in this study, provided the most accurate and efficient method of analyzing pronghorn rumen samples. Fecal analysis results compared favorably to the other methods used. The known diet study indicated that differential digestion of epidermal fragments may occur under certain conditions.

84. Smith, A. D.; Beale, D. M.; Doell, D. D. 1965. Browse preferences of pronghorn antelope in southwestern Utah. In: Trefethen, James B., ed. Transactions of the thirtieth North American wildlife and natural resources conference; 1965 March 8-10; Washington, DC. Washington, DC: Wildlife Management Institute: 136-141.

Six antelope were fed 16 species of browse plants common on desert ranges of Utah for a period of six days on the Desert Experimental Range. Ample amounts of all species were available so that free choice could be expressed. Big sagebrush, black sagebrush, and juniper provided the major part of the diet. More than half was provided by big sagebrush. Nutrient values of the diet were computed using digestion coefficients determined with mule deer and sheep. The values thus obtained were well in excess of accepted standards for domestic sheep. Unless competition from livestock seriously reduces the volume of sagebrush available to antelope, a low plane of nutrition during winter does not appear to be a factor in the productivity of this species in western Utah.

85. Smith, Courtney Bingham. 1984. Analysis of grazing effects and site factors in relation to grazing use of salt desert shrub vegetation, Desert Experimental Range, Utah, 1938-1974. Logan, UT: Utah State University. 243 p. Dissertation.

Data from a U.S. Forest Service study at the Desert Experimental Range were analyzed to determine the effects of season and intensity of grazing treatments on production of native range vegetation. Analyses included evaluation of trends in plant species' production over time and stratification by either soil or plant community type. Preliminary analyses consisted of plant community classification, correlation of soil and plant community types, and correlation of species' yields to seasonal precipitation. Palatable shrubs declined with late winter grazing compared to early winter use. The greatest relative increases for *Artemisia spinescens* under dormant season grazing occurred where *Atriplex confertifolia* declined. This suggests a return of plant community composition towards pre-settlement conditions. Declines for *Ceratoides lanata* under late winter grazing were most pronounced at heavy stocking rates on comparatively fine-textured soils. Interactive effects of heavy use and prolonged below-normal precipitation, or flooding damage apparently contributed to this decline. *Atriplex confertifolia* tended to increase where production of *Ceratoides lanata* was reduced, but these increases were short-lived. Sensitivity of *Atriplex confertifolia* to drought limited its ability to replace more valuable forage species. Grasses generally showed little difference in yield among treatments, or they increased with heavy use and in communities dominated by shrubs. This applied as well to *Oryzopsis hymenoides*, which was utilized heavily at all stocking rates. This use was apparently not excessive during early winter, and late winter grazing occurred early enough in the growing season to allow for plant recovery. *Sporobolus* spp. increased with early-heavy grazing but declined with late-heavy use. Drought and late-heavy grazing probably reduced survival of these species. Trends in plant production over time showed few treatment differences. Trends for *Artemisia spinescens* differed among seasonal treatments, but only the declines under late winter users were consistent. *Ceratoides lanata* showed short-term changes in yield over time but no consistent long-term trend with any treatment. More complex models and experimental testing of the effects of seasonal precipitation on plant species' production may be needed to isolate long-term trends in yield.

86. Stewart, George; Cottam, W. P.; Hutchings, Selar S. 1940. Influence of unrestricted grazing on northern salt desert plant associations in western Utah. Journal of Agricultural Research 60(5): 289-316.

The vegetation in Wah Wah Valley, Utah, which has been grazed for about 70 years, and severely so for about 50 years, is compared with that in the nearby Pine Valley where, owing to the scarcity of stock water, grazing use was heavy only when snow was available until about 20 years ago, when watering places were artificially developed. Pine Valley is the site of the Desert Experimental Range. The plant cover of these two neighboring valleys—comparable in size, in physiographic features, in soils, and in forage-plant associations—differed mainly as a result of the duration and intensity of livestock grazing to which they had been subjected. In order to compare the effects on vegetation of these two types of grazing use, the density, kind, and condition of the forage plants in the two valleys as well as the prevalent soil conditions, were studied on a long transect across each valley. Palatable perennial grasses, formerly conspicuous in all the desert shrub associations, are few in number and low in vigor where the grazing has been severe during the protracted period of approximately 50 years. In comparison with those of low palatability, species of high palatability have suffered (1) a greater loss in density of plant cover, (2) a higher plant mortality, (3) a greater decrease in reproduction, and (4) a sharper decline in general vigor. Palatable shrubs such as winterfat, shadscale, spiny hop-sage, and black sagebrush have also suffered in the same respects as have the grasses under prolonged heavy grazing. Of the forage shrubs, on which ring counts were made, very few plants were less than about 20 years of age. Grasses also showed low reproduction during a long period of years, although the length of the period was not susceptible to accurate determination. The root systems of the desert forage species studied were found to be largely limited to the upper 30 cm of soil where the salt content rarely exceeds 1,000 parts per million. The root systems of big sagebrush and spiny hop-sage extend much deeper than this. Associations in which these species are dominant are limited to areas where even the subsoils have a low salt content. The naturally sparse plant cover, when thinned and weakened by unrestricted grazing, has permitted heavy wind erosion, and on a few of the worst areas, the beginning of dune formation.

On heavily grazed areas, small rabbitbrush—low in palatability to livestock and once rare on the desert—has replaced, to an alarming extent, the more palatable species, but is still rare where the palatable species are vigorous. Russian-thistle, introduced to the desert two decades ago, is not a serious competitor in vigorous shrub communities; however, on heavily grazed areas that are depleted of vegetation it has taken possession and apparently retards reproduction of desert shrubs. Impoverishment of desert forage, attributed by many to the drought of 1928-1935, was not so markedly apparent after the drought of 1897-1904, which was of as long duration and, measured in total precipitation, more severe. The evidence gained from the study of these plant associations does not support the theory that drought is the sole or even the chief cause of present deterioration and depletion of the range. Instead, it points unmistakably to unrestricted grazing as the chief cause of loss of grazing values, invasion of inferior species, and the gradual crowding out of the most palatable range plants. The data show clearly that the heavy utilization of the forage by livestock must be relaxed in order to provide for restoration of the range to normal producing power and for its subsequent maintenance. The original presence of accessible stock water in Wah Wah Valley permitted heavy range use in the fall, spring, and winter. The artificial development about 20 years ago of stock water in Pine Valley, formerly grazed only when snow was available, has permitted heavy use in fall, spring, and winter since that time. The result during the last few years has been deterioration of forage plants because of overuse. Permanent and vigorous forage production on the winter ranges will require the sort of range management that avoids complete utilization of the current year's growth and that will give some relaxation in the degree of use during fall and spring. Development of wells and other stock-watering places needs to be accompanied by control and management of livestock to keep the new watering places from becoming centers of yet further forage deterioration.

87. Stewart, George; Hutchings, Selar S. 1936. The point-observation plot (square-root density) method of vegetation survey. American Society of Agronomy Journal 28(9): 714-726.

This paper explains the working of the point-observation-plot method of vegetation survey which evolved over a period of 4 years. Data were collected, in part, at the Desert Experimental Range. The following formal description is deemed necessary because this method is already highly useful and has been tried sufficiently by many agencies concerned with the measurement of range plant growth to show its practicability. Its application extends throughout the fields of range management, pasture management, agronomy, and soil erosion. It provides definitely quantitative data instead of merely qualitative. The improved method is founded on the technique long used by plant breeders to obtain reliable, preliminary field test results of large numbers of strains. It includes randomization and replication of plots and, lends itself readily to statistical analysis. It has been modified to include many phases of the timber survey and certain refinements of the range reconnaissance survey long used by the Forest Service and other organizations.

88. Stewart, George; Keller, Wesley. 1936. Correlation method for ecology as exemplified by studies of native desert vegetation. Ecology 17(3): 500-514.

This study is an attempt to determine the various relationships between species on the northern shrub desert of western Utah including the Desert Experimental Range. When the variables employed are limited to species, the values obtained are consistently rather small, over half of the total being non-significant. The other coefficients, however, are so definitely and so consistently significant as to leave little doubt that a major species is distinctly influenced as a result of the presence of the others. When all of the significant correlations between each pair of species were grouped, there was a marked tendency for all the coefficients in each group to have the same sign. The relationships between any such pair of species are not randomly distributed indicating that definite factors of considerable constancy are causing these relationships. The complete interpretation for this fact cannot be established from the data although several likely explanations suggest themselves each having something to do with the intensity of competition.

89. Sykes, Dwane Jay. 1964. The availability of soil moisture to plants. Ames, IA: Iowa State University. 147 p. Dissertation.

Experiments with continuous and interrupted soil columns have shown that the field capacity of soil moisture is dependent on downward capillary moisture movement in addition to gravitational drainage. Field capacity retention was shown to be partially dependent on the depth of wetting. This deviation from the generally accepted concept is explained by dependence of the hydraulic gradient on the depth of wetting. The thesis is advanced that the major limiting factor determining the permanent wilting percentage is the rate of moisture movement through the soil to the plant roots and that, in contrast to the 15-atmosphere concept, a xeric species or a drought-hardened plant may withstand high soil moisture tension, perhaps equal to its cellular osmotic potential, while soil moisture moves slowly to its roots. Such xeric or drought hardened plants may show a lower permanent wilting percentage and a much higher permanent wilting tension than would mesic plants, especially on a soil having relatively rapid moisture crawl. The results of this study conducted, in part at the Desert Experimental Range, indicate that the generally accepted concepts of both field capacity and the permanent wilting percentage, as commonly stated, are inadequate and are neither as valid nor universal as has been presumed.

90. Tew, Ronald K.; Kitchen, Stanley G.; Holmgren, Ralph C. 1997. Soil survey—Desert Experimental Range, Utah. Gen. Tech. Rep. INT-347. Ogden, UT: U.S. Department of Agriculture, Forest Service, Intermountain Research Station. 22 p.

Soils were mapped on the 22,533 ha Desert Experimental Range, Utah, to determine the kind, extent, and distribution of major soils and soil groups, the type of vegetation associated with each soil group, and the correlation between herbage production and soil groups. The results indicated that Desert Experimental Range soils are primarily Haplocalcids, Torriothents, and Torrifluvents. They occur within

the Temperate Desert and Temperate Steppe climatic types. Annual herbage production averages 250 kg per ha per year. High production years yield twice the average, often with many annual herbs, while low production years yield less than half the average. Species composition differs greatly on dissimilar soils and over time, but total production is similar for Haplocalcids, Torriothents, and Torrifluvents.

91. Thacker, Randall K.; Flinders, Jerran T.; Blackwell, Boyd H.; Smith, H. Duane. 1995. Comparison and use of four techniques for censusing three sub-species of kit fox. Provo, UT: Final report, a cooperative contract study between: wildlife section, Utah Division of Wildlife Resources and Brigham Young University. 72 p.

Population indices can provide reliable estimates of abundance for kit fox. Estimates of kit fox abundance varied seasonally depending on the method of census. They are most effective when conducted during July or August when juveniles are active. Kit fox abundance by censusing is correlated with availability of the leporid prey base. Kit fox population index is determined by dividing the number of stations with fox tracks by the number of station examined in the test period. The research was performed, in part, at the Desert Experimental Range.

92. Thorderson, Larry G. 1987. Restoring estimability in designs with missing cells: and application to the analysis of livestock grazing patterns in southwestern Utah. Provo, UT: Brigham Young University. 78 p. Thesis.

Missing-cell and data-imbalance problems and the proper procedures for completing an analysis in the face of their presence is discussed in the course of presenting an analysis of a large set of plant cover measurement. The data that was examined for this study was collected at the Desert Experimental Range. Techniques for finding estimable contrasts are used to perform valid statistical significance tests. Statistically significant interactions involving grazing treatments, plant community, and soil type found were discussed.

93. Welch, Bruce L.; Briggs, Steven F.; Young, Stanford A. 1994. Pine Valley Ridge source—a superior selected germplasm of black sagebrush. Res. Pap. INT-474. Ogden, UT: U.S. Department of Agriculture, Forest Service, Intermountain Research Station. 9 p.

This document establishes the basis for the release of Pine Valley Ridge source, a superior selected germplasm of black sagebrush (*Artemisia nova*). This ecotype of black sagebrush, a tetraploid (2n = 36), was collected near the northeast corner of the Intermountain Research Station's Desert Experimental Range, Millard County, UT. Its energy, crude protein, phosphorus, and carotene levels exceed those of most winter forages and will increase nutrients in the winter diets of pronghorn (*Antilocapra americana*), domestic sheep (*Ovis aries*), mule deer (*Odocoileus hemianus hemianus*), and cattle (*Bos bovine*). This black sagebrush is better adapted to drier sites than previously released germplasms: Gordon Creek (Wyoming big sagebrush, *A. tridentata* ssp. *wyomingensis*) and 'Hobble Creek' (mountain big sagebrush, *A. t.* ssp. *vaseyana*). Wintering mule deer preferred Pine Valley Ridge source over other black sagebrush germplasms tested. On its native site, Pine Valley Ridge is sought out by pronghorn year-round and by domestic sheep during winter. Cattle have been observed eating it during winter. Pine Valley Ridge can be established and maintained over a wide geographic range on sites with the following characteristics: mean annual precipitation of 7 to 16 inches; deep to shallow, well-drained soils; soil clay content under 22 percent; soil pH from 6.6 to 8.8; and a frost-free period of at least 75 days. Pine Valley Ridge can be established by direct seeding on properly prepared seedbeds, by transplanting bare-root or containerized stock, or by a technique termed "mother plant" in which shrubs transplanted on a 50 by 50 foot grid produce seeds to fill in the openings.

94. Wells, Gail. 2009. Experimental forests and ranges, 100 years of research success stories. Gen. Tech. Rep. FPL-GTR-182. Madison, WI: U.S. Department of Agriculture, Forest Service, Forest Products Laboratory. 29 p.

For a century, scientists of the USDA Forest Service have been reading the language of the land on a comprehensive network of experimental forests and ranges. These 81 sites encompass a rich variety of forest and grassland ecosystems across the United States and Puerto Rico. They range from boreal forest to tropical forest to peat-bog deciduous forest (Marcell Experimental Forest in Minnesota) to semi-arid chaparral (San Dimas Experimental Forest in California) to dry desert (Desert Experimental Range [DER] in Utah). In 2008, Forest Service Research and Development celebrated the Centennial Anniversary of these Experimental Forests and Ranges. This publication celebrates the many scientists who, over the course of decades, conducted the long-term-studies that began and are continuing to shed light on important natural resource issues. Story suggestions were solicited from the Experimental Forest and Range Working Group and were selected to demonstrate the array of research issues being addressed on these living laboratories. Gathering a wealth of information from her interviews with scientists, Gail Wells proceeded to write these 'wonderful success stories from 100 years of research.' Studies established decades ago on many of these sites are still going strong. Experimental forests and ranges provide a valuable, long-term stream of information about the

USDA Forest Service Gen. Tech. Rep. RMRS-GTR-312WWW. 2013

44

land and its resources. Over the years, researchers have built an impressive body of science to support good land management and further understanding of natural processes. Their research sheds light on many important questions. These experimental forests serve as living laboratories that help connect the future to the past. The Desert Experimental Range is highlighted in a section titled "Old Research Sheds Light on New Questions" where Stan Kitchen, the DER Scientist-In-Charge provided the following information:

Composed of 22,500 hectares (about 55,600 acres) of mostly treeless salt-desert shrubland, the DER is the largest of all the Forest Service's experimental forests and ranges. Its sparse vegetation and minimal precipitation make it typical of an ecosystem that is widespread across the vast Great Basin, an internally drained region covering about 55 million hectares (135 million acres) of the Intermountain West. More than half the land in the Great Basin is administered by the USDI Bureau of Land Management, and most of that is divided into grazing allotments for domestic sheep and cattle. Grazing has been a dominant land use since European-American settlers arrived in the mid-19th century. Historically, ranchers paid little attention to management or protection of the resource, and by the early 20th century the range had lost much of its ecosystem function and its capacity to support livestock. The DER was set aside in 1933 as a place to investigate the economic and ecological impacts of grazing. In 1934 and 1935, the first researchers established 20 paddocks of 100–130 hectares (240–320 acres) each, of which 16 had two, 4,000-m^2 (1-acre) fenced "exclosures," or control areas where the animals couldn't graze. Grazing treatments in these paddocks have been used to test the long-term effects of various combinations of grazing intensity and season. Changes in vegetation are still being monitored today on permanent plots in these paddocks and their associated exclosures. They've provided a long-term look at plant succession in response to grazing and also a look at year-to-year variations in response to climate.

95. West, Neil E. 1979. Survival patterns of major perennials in salt desert shrub communities of southwestern Utah. Journal of Range Management 32(6): 442-445.

Chart quadrat records periodically taken at the Desert Experimental Range in southwestern Utah over 34 years were examined for evidence of establishment and survival of eight major perennial plant species. A set of seedlings that became established in 1935-1937 were followed until 1968-1970. Relatively few individuals have died since the second year after establishment. There were few significant differences between the survival of plants in the grazed versus ungrazed plots.

96. West, N. E. 1983. Intermountain salt-desert shrubland. In: West, N. E., ed. Temperate deserts and semi-deserts. Amsterdam, The Netherlands: 375-397.

This chapter describes the salt-desert shrublands of North America emphasizing lands dominated by shrubs and half-shrubs of the chenopod family. Their dominance is usually associated with halomorphic soils and the area is often called the salt desert shrub type. Some of the data were gathered from the Desert Experimental Range. These lands have low natural productivity, little open water, and limited potential for intensive agriculture. The major uses have been for range livestock grazing, mining of accumulated minerals, and military testing and maneuvers.

97. Wood, Benjamin W. 1966. An ecological life history of budsage. Provo, UT: Brigham Young University. 85 p. Thesis.

This study was conducted from 1963 to 1965 in western Millard County, UT, and adjacent White Pine County, Nevada. Specific study sites were located at seven locations where budsage grows in Pine, Antelope, Snake, and Hamlin Valleys. Most of the sites in Pine Valley were on the Desert Experimental Range. The study sites were selected as being representative of the different communities in which budsage occurs. Summer dormancy and root growth patterns indicate methods of adaptation. Grazing records show that late winter grazing could be very detrimental to *A. spinescens* growth and survival.

98. Wood, Benjamin W.; Brotherson, Jack D. 1986. Ecological adaptation and grazing response of budsage (*Artemisia spinescens*) in southwestern Utah. In: McArthur, E. Durant; Welch, Bruce L., comps. Proceedings—symposium on the biology of *Artemisia* and *Chrysothamnus*; 1984 July 9-13; Gen. Tech. Rep. INT-200. Provo, UT. Ogden, UT: U.S. Department of Agriculture, Forest Service, Intermountain Research Station: 75-92.

Several *Artemisia spinescens* sites representing different plant communities and different grazing histories were studied to investigate physical adaptations and the influence of grazing on this species. Summer dormancy and root growth patterns indicate methods of adaptation. Grazing records at the Desert Experimental Range show that late winter grazing could be very detrimental to *A. spinescens* growth and survival.

99. Zhang, Yongguang; Moran, M. Susan; Nearing, Mark A.; Ponce-Campos, Guillermo E.; Huete, Alfredo R.; Buda, Anthony R.; Bosch, David D.; Gunter, Stacey A.; Kitchen, Stanley G.; McNab, W. Henry; Morgan, Jack A.; McClaran, Mitchel P.; Montoya, Diane S.; Peters, Debra P. C.; Starks, Patrick J. 2013. Extreme precipitation patterns reduced terrestrial ecosystem production across biomes Journal of Geophysical Research—Biogeosciences 118:1-10.

Precipitation regimes are predicted to shift to more extreme patterns that are characterized by more heavy rainfall events and longer dry intervals, yet their ecological impacts on vegetation production remain uncertain across biomes in natural climatic conditions. This in situ study investigated the effects of novel climatic conditions on aboveground net primary production (ANPP) by combining a greenness index from satellite measurements and climatic records during 2000 to 2009 from 11 long-term experimental sites including the Desert Experimental Range in multiple biomes and climates. Results showed that extreme precipitation patterns decreased the sensitivity of ANPP to total annual precipitation (PT), at the regional and decadal scales, leading to decreased rain-use efficiency (by 20% on average) across biomes. Relative decreases in ANPP were greatest for arid grassland (16%) and Mediterranean forest (20%), and less for mesic grassland and temperate forest (3%). The co-occurrence of heavy rainfall events and longer dry intervals caused greater water stress conditions that resulted in reduced vegetation production. A new generalized model was developed using a function of both PT and an index of precipitation extremes, and improved predictions of the sensitivity of ANPP to changes in precipitation patterns. The results clearly suggest that extreme precipitation patterns have substantial and complex effects on vegetation production across biomes, and are as important as total annual precipitation. With predictions of more extreme weather events, forecasts of ecosystem production should consider these non-linear responses to altered extreme precipitation patterns associated with climate change.

Chronological Index

1934 – 1939: 79, 87, 88

1940 – 1949: 46, 73, 86

1950 – 1959: 38, 47, 48, 49, 50, 53, 54

1960 – 1969: 11, 12, 17, 19, 32, 51, 52, 68, 80, 84, 89, 97

1970 – 1979: 05, 08, 13, 14, 20, 36, 37, 44, 45, 55, 72, 76, 83, 95

1980 – 1989: 06, 07, 09, 10, 15, 16, 22, 23, 24, 25, 26, 27, 28, 29, 35, 42, 43, 56, 70, 75, 77, 78, 82, 85, 92, 96, 98

1990 – 1999: 02, 03, 04, 18, 21, 33, 34, 39, 40, 41, 58, 59, 61, 62, 63, 69, 90, 91, 93

2000 – 2013: 01, 30, 31, 57, 60, 64, 65, 66, 67, 71, 74, 81, 94, 99

Publication Type Index

Journal Article: 02, 04, 06, 07, 08, 11, 12, 13, 14, 15, 17, 18, 21, 24, 25, 26, 30, 31, 32, 34, 41, 46, 47, 48, 53, 55, 56, 70, 73, 79, 81, 82, 86, 87, 88, 95, 99

Book Chapter: 78, 96

Symposium Proceedings: 22, 23, 27, 28, 29, 39, 40, 42, 43, 45, 51, 52, 57, 58, 59, 60, 61, 63, 71, 75, 76, 80, 84, 98

Federal Agency Research Paper, Circular, Bulletin, leaflet, General Technical Report, Other Report: 01, 09, 10, 16, 35, 44, 49, 50, 54, 62, 64, 65, 66, 67, 68, 74, 90, 93, 94

State Agency Report: 33, 91

Dissertation (PhD): 03, 05, 69, 85, 89

Thesis (MS): 19, 20, 36, 37, 38, 72, 77, 83, 92, 97

Subject Matter Index

Bird Ecology: 18, 72

Community Ecology: 16, 19, 20, 21, 34, 38, 40, 57, 58, 60, 61, 63, 76, 81, 88, 90, 95, 96

Disturbance (Grazing) Ecology and Succession: 02, 03, 04, 05, 06, 07, 16, 20, 21, 22, 23, 28, 29, 30, 32, 38, 40, 51, 54, 58, 59, 61, 69, 70, 75, 76, 85, 86, 98

Geography, Geology, Climate: 04, 09, 19, 20, 21, 43, 81, 90, 99

Historical and Site Description: 01, 10, 26, 42, 57, 62, 64, 65, 66, 67, 68, 71, 94

Livestock Management: 41, 45, 46, 47, 48, 49, 50, 51, 52, 54, 73

Mammal Ecology: 11, 13, 14, 15, 24, 25, 27, 36, 56, 77, 78, 84, 91

Methodology: 12, 18, 28, 30, 34, 53, 55, 63, 79, 82, 83, 87, 88, 89, 91, 92

Plant Autecology: 15, 16, 19, 37, 93, 97, 98

Plant Taxonomy or Status: 33, 35

Restoration Ecology: 16, 17, 74, 80, 93

Soil Biology and Ecology: 05, 06, 07, 08, 16, 31, 39, 44, 60, 69, 70, 89, 90

Weed Ecology: 34, 39, 60, 61

Author Index[1]

Adams MB: 01

Alados CL: 02

Alzérreca-Angelo H: 03, 04

Anderson DC: 05, 06, 07, 08

Anderson RE: 09

Baugh T: 10

Beale DM: 11, 12, 13, 14, (24, 25, 84)

Behan B: 15

Belnap J: (31)

Blackwell BH: (91)

Blaisdell JP: 16

Bleak AT: 17

Bosch, DD: (81, 99)

Boyer KC: (75)

Bradford DF: 18

Bresloff, C: (81)

Brewster SF Jr: 19, (44)

Briggs SF: (93)

Brotherson JD: (98)

Buda, AR: (81, 99)

Canterbury GE: (18)

Carlson SL: (57)

Chambers JC 20, 21

Chavez PS Jr: (82)

---

[1] Numbers refer to bibliographic entries; non-senior authorship is listed in parentheses.

Clary WP: 22, 23, 24, 25, 26, 27, 28, 29, (40, 78)

Cottam WP: (86)

De Soyza AG: 30

Doell DD: (84)

Duda JJ: 31

Eamus D: (81)

Eckert RE Jr: (17)

Ellison L: 32

Emlen JM: (02, 31, 34)

Flinders JT: (78, 91)

Franklin MA (Ben): 33

Franson SE: (18)

Freeman DC: (02, 31), 34

Frischknecht NC: (17)

Galt D: (41)

Garcia JR: (56)

Gehring D: (82)

Goodrich S: 35

Green JS: 36

Guerra SL: 37

Gunter SA: (81, 99)

Hall DB: (58, 59)

Harper KT: (06, 07), 38, 39, 40, (70, 75)

Havsted KM: (30)

Haws A: (75)

Heggem DT: (18)

Herrick JE: (30)

Holechek JL: 41

Holmgren RC: (06, 16, 25, 26, 27, 28, 29), 42, 43, 44, 45, (53, 82, 90)

Huete A: (81, 99)

Hutchings SS: (45), 46, 47, 48, 49, 50, 51, 52, 53, 54, (86, 87)

Huxman TE: (81)

Jorgensen CD: 55, 56

Jorgensen GL: (60, 61, 63)

Keller W: (88)

Kitchen SG: (04, 31, 39), 57, 58, 59, 60, 61, 62, 63, (81, 90, 99)

Klade RJ: 64, 65, 66, 67

Laycock WA: 68

Loughry L: (1)

Marble JR: 69, 70, (75)

McArthur ED: (62, 63), 71

McArthur LD: 72

McClaran MP: (81, 99)

McGinnies WJ: 73

McNab WH: (81, 99)

Miller GR: (18)

Molinar F: (41)

Monsen SB: 74

Montoya DS: (81, 99)

Montante J: (31)

Moran MS: (81, 99)

Morgan JA: (81, 99)

Neale AC: (18, 30)

Nearing MA: (99)

Nelson DL: 75

Norton BE: (21), 76

O'Neal GT: 77, 78

Peters DPC: (81, 99)

Pickford GD: 79

Plaugher L: (01)

Plummer AP: (17), 80

Ponce-Campos GE: 81, (99)

Robinove CJ: 82

Rushforth SR: (07, 08)

Sadler EJ: (81)

Scalley TH: (81)

Schupp EW: (04)

Scotter GW: (11)

Shandruck LJ: 83

Shaw NL: (74)

Smith AD: (12, 13, 14), 84

Smith CB: 85

Smith HD: (55, 56, 91)

Sobek E: (31)

Starks PJ: (99)

Stevens R: (74)

Stewart G: (54, 79), 86, 87, 88

Sykes DJ: 89

Tallent-Hallsel N: (30)

Tew RK: 90

Thacker RK: 91

Thomas M: (41)

Thorderson LG: 92

Tracy M: (31)

Van Buren R: (39)

Van Zee JW: (30)

Wachocki B: (02)

Wagstaff FJ (40)

Weber DJ: (75)

Welch BL: (15), 93

Wells G: 94

West NE: 95, 96

Whitford WG: (30)

Wood BW: 97, 98

Young SA: (93)

Zak JC: (31)

Zhang, Y: (81), 99

USDA Forest Service Gen. Tech. Rep. RMRS-GTR-312WWW. 2013

52

To learn more about RMRS publications or search our online titles:

www.fs.fed.us/rm/publications

www.treesearch.fs.fed.us